Our First Fifty Years

Life in the Wilderness

To Brett & Susie –
May you enjoy some
adventures in life –
Dick & KayD Johnson

Dick and KayD Johnson

First Printing, 2013
United States of America

Printed by:
Medicus Graphics Center
Los Angeles, California, USA

ISBN: 978-0-9773108-0-7

Cover Design by Manuel Rios / Medicus Graphics Center

Contact information:
Dick and KayD Publications
Dick and KayD Johnson
P.O. Box 140049
Salcha, Alaska 99714
email: dick907@yahoo.com

This book is dedicated to

Our sons,
Robert and Jeff

Our grandchildren,
Jeffrey, Crystalynn and Amanda

Our great-grandchildren,
Calista, Jason and Tyler

THE BEGINNING

Many times we have been asked just how Dick and I met and why do we live so far away from the normal lifestyle of society. Well, our relationship started back in February 1960 when I was with a friend, Bill McCloskey, who had stopped to see his old neighbors. While we were at their house we got involved with a card game of Canasta which was popular back then. Soon a young man came in to visit Bill after seeing his car in the driveway. The visitor, Dick, was introduced to me and I realized that I knew of him and had been trying to meet him for some time but was told that he was not interested in girls right now. Dick's interests were in cars, hiking, mountains, hunting and fishing.

Well, it just happened to be a leap year and I figured why not just ask Dick for a date and see what happens—nothing ventured, nothing gained as I always said! So about fifteen minutes later I mentioned to everyone around the card table that this was a leap year and it was alright for girls to ask guys out and then I proceeded to say directly to Dick, "You ought to marry me!" His immediate reply was, "It sounds great to me." Well, I almost fainted then, but we started to see each other every day for the next two weeks, always with Bill along as chaperone.

We drove into the local mountains to work on his car and have picnics in the woods. We spent many days in the desert shooting guns at targets, something I had never done in my life. But we only had one real date and that was to go roller skating at the local rink after dinner out. Bill and his girlfriend, Judy, went with us on this date too.

Each evening we would sit in Denney's restaurant drinking coffee until the wee hours of the morning and talking about our dreams, families and futures. Finally we decided that we really did want to spend our lives together and Dick even proposed to me before leaving for overseas duty in Japan for 16 months on February 27, 1960. Yes, I found out he was in the US Navy and still had almost 2 years of service to complete. That was alright with me as I still had to complete high school and graduate. We made a commitment to get married after he returned home from Japan.

Then we went to meet each others parents which did not go to well at the time. It seems they felt unanimously that we were both crazy young fools that had no idea what we were doing but we were adamant and have been together ever since. I was supposed to go to Dick's parents one night a week for dinner and a visit so they could get to know me while he was gone overseas. A few years later our parents finally agreed that it just might last and have been avid supporters of our relationship since. Sometimes it takes a while to get parents to come around to our way of thinking!!

So Dick went to Japan and as his parents drove off with him in the car my heart was breaking as we would not see each other for another 16 months. We wrote letters to each other every single day for the next 16 months which was terrific as it gave us a better chance to get to know the deep inner thinking of each other. We discussed everything under the sun from relationships, marriage, children, finances, pet peeves we have, and so much more in real depth. It is much easier to have these discussions when you are writing as you are not so busy with trying to concentrate from all the hugging and kissing part of a dating scene. By the time Dick returned to the USA we really had a deep knowledge of each other and our families. I was busy with a part time job, attending high school and raising my younger brother. My brother and I moved in with Dick's parents who were empty nesters at that time for almost one year before Dick came home.

In January 1961 I graduated from high school and went on working full time as planned to prepare for our wedding. I had been planning ahead all this time and getting things ready to set up housekeeping for us by purchasing some used furniture which I put into storage with my things that were already stored away. So by the time we married I had purchased all our kitchen needs, two bedroom sets and a few extra things. We are still using the same pots, pans, utensils, silverware and such from that time. Our sons grew up with the twin bedroom set I bought from the Johnsons. We do tend to keep things forever and like using items from long ago.

Then on June 15, 1961 I awoke to someone kissing me and it was Dick home from Japan. Wow, you could not have found a happier person right then!! He was home almost a month early and we were so elated. Luckily I had all the wedding plans done and paid for with invitations for about 50 people ready for the mail, church reserved, and reception arranged in the recreation hall at the pool side in the mobile home park where Mr. and Mrs. Johnson were living. I had purchased my dress and reserved tuxedos for the guys and only needed to arrange for flowers. Now I had the next month to just enjoy my future husband.

To say the least we had a most wonderful time together even going out on another real date to the drive in theater to see "GONE WITH THE WIND", a very popular movie at that time. Dick and I spent time working on his Jeep station wagon getting it ready for camping and we took our first trip in the wagon over the 4th of July to visit Dick's older sister and family. Then on up into the High Sierra Mountains along the south fork of the Kern River in Kennedy Meadows where Dick loved to go fishing and hunting. Dick really wanted to share this area with me and I fell in love with the place immediately. While on this trip Dick shared with me the fact that all the money he had sent home to be put into a savings account for starting our marriage was gone. It seems his parents had spent all of it so we were essentially broke except for his final paycheck and my job. After a long discussion we decided not to worry about all this but just continue on with our plans. Dick was not going to look for a job until after our wedding because we wanted to have a few days to ourselves for a honeymoon. We thought we may just go camping in Kennedy Meadows for our honeymoon as it was much more economical for us.

The big day came and we had a wonderful wedding July 31, 1961, in a tiny church in North Hollywood where many more people came than expected, followed by a nice reception at the mobile home park where Dick's parents lived. The only sad part of the day was that neither of my parents were present but we did have both my brothers and many other relatives with us. Dick and I were off before midnight in our Jeep wagon for two weeks camping.

After only one week we were getting concerned about finding a place to live and a job for Dick so we decided to return to the San Fernando Valley and start looking now. It only took us two days to find a nice two bedroom apartment that we could afford and we had a very understanding ex-military man as manager who gave us a good deal without a deposit so we paid the remaining three weeks of the first months rent. Now we had a place to stay but not enough money to get our furniture out of storage and pay all the deposits for the utilities so we made a big decision to get the water turned on, empty our storage unit and live with our camping gear until next month when we could turn on the lights and gas. It was fun as we cooked with our Coleman stove on top of the kitchen stove and had two kerosene lamps for lights. The living room was completely empty except for a large picture of Mount Fuji over the fireplace and an old, Persian area rug on the floor. We spent most of our time at the kitchen table or in bed. The next month we had all utilities working and were looking at some cheap living room furniture which we couldn't purchase until just before Thanksgiving but it would be nice to have a place for company to sit besides the kitchen table.

Dick started looking for work immediately and had a job within two weeks at Lockheed Aircraft Corporation but with one BIG problem. Dick was given a list of minimum essential tools needed for the job and we went to Sears to price them. We found ourselves about ten dollars short of being able to buy the tools so we had to go ask his parents for a ten dollar loan until payday. Wow, that turned out to be quite nasty as we were told how irresponsible we were, but in the end he got the money and we went directly to Sears for the tools. Dick was happy to be back to work and in on a great big project that gave him a lot of overtime through the winter months which came in handy financially for us.

By September we had discovered we were going to have a baby and after checking with Dick's medical plan at work we found out that we would not be covered because the baby would be born before Dick's first ten months of employment. That was a real blow to us so we started putting away money for the birth of our first son. This was also the month in which my younger brother returned to us after spending the summer with our dad in Catalina. Dave, my brother, was happy to see his room all set up ready for him to move into. Dave was now getting ready for high school and having a bit more trouble with some of his studies but Dick was a great help to him. We were also trying to teach Dave to drive a standard transmission vehicle which was fun. Several times we drove up to the mountains to camp for a weekend and get away from the big city.

The next thing we knew it was the holiday season 1961. I was excited to have the living room all furnished and wanted to have family here for Christmas. We had fun purchasing all our first ornaments, lights and tree. It was my very first big meal for company with turkey and all the trimmings. I wanted it to be very special and come out looking like a photo in Better Homes and Gardens!! The meal went well and we had a wonderful time. I was so proud of doing this for Dick's parents. We had given Dick's dad an electric HO model train set as he always wanted one but no one took him seriously and we will cherish his facial expression forever. Such surprise and happiness!! Dick's parents gave us our set of hammered andirons and metal wood basket for the fireplace that we still use to this day.

The winter passed quickly with Dick working a lot of overtime and I finally had to quit my job due to pregnancy. I was huge and having problems with swelling legs and feet. It was great fun to find and purchase a used baby bed and dresser which we painted and put decals on. Then we bought a new mattress for the baby bed. My friends had a baby shower for me and we purchased a few other essential items needed. Eventually the day came when we thought we were having a baby and we went to the hospital where I was prepped. Then we sat through the night with contractions when our baby decided he was not ready and turned around. The doctor wanted me to stay but I felt fine and said we could not afford to just sit here so I went home. Thank heaven I went home because that was May 10th and he was not born until June 3rd. We felt so lucky to have a very healthy, good looking baby boy. We took him on his first camping trip over the July 4th weekend.

By the time our son was born we had put a down payment on some property in Kennedy Meadows in the High Sierra Mountains which had a $24 per month payment to the owner. So, on our first camping trip with our new baby we drove to OUR LAND and we took along some lumber and proceeded to build a small 12x12 foot A-frame cabin. We were living in a tent during this construction but summer time was quite lovely with moderate temperatures. Dick had a two week vacation and after the vacation was over we had decided that we really wanted to live in the wilderness and raise our children in that lifestyle. So upon our return to the city and work Dick gave his notice to quit by the middle of September. We spent the next two months purchasing all the things we thought we would need including groceries to live for the coming year in the wilderness. That would all be paid for and allow Dick time to job hunt without worries. We had enough money to make our property payments until spring time. We were young, healthy, hard workers and had the world by the tail what else did we need to survive?

When we announced to our parents our plans to move the explosion could have been heard in Europe! To say the least, they were not happy and considered us to be very irresponsible, stupid and much more than can be printed in a book. In fact, our parents disowned us for quite a while until we proved we had made a good decision for ourselves. We tried to tell them we were not going to the moon but only a 4 hour drive away which made no difference to them at all. The only real down side of our move was that my younger brother did not want to go back a half year in school if he moved with us and so he decided to live with our dad for the remaining years of his schooling. We really missed him but understood his position so well.

A friend of Dick's from his time in the Navy had come back to the USA upon discharge shortly before our son was born. Hank did not have any family in the west and we invited him to stay with us until he could find a job and get settled on his own. He shared the bedroom with my brother Dave. Hank was hired soon at Lockheed Aircraft just like Dick and life was quite compatible between all of us. When we decided to move to the mountains Hank suggested he stay in our apartment with all of our furniture for at least one year just in case we had to move back to the city. That would give him a place to stay and he would cover all the rent and utilities during this period. Well that was a great idea for us and we took him up on his offer. By the time the year was up we knew we were going to make it in the wilderness and we moved our household goods to the town where Dick worked and put it all in storage until we could build us a house to move our belongings into.

That move was the beginning of my education in wilderness living. You must know that I had never even camped a day in my life until meeting Dick, I was a real city girl. We were lucky to get all of Dick's grandfather's hand tools from his farming days in Pennsylvania; many of the items were totally unfamiliar to us. We had purchased a couple of big wash tubs, a scrub board, two big buckets, kerosene lamps, a woodstove for heat and were given a 55 gallon barrel for water and two flat irons. We found a good buy on an old 20 inch propane cook stove and small bookcase for cupboards so now we were set for housekeeping. It only took me a couple of days to organize all our things into the small cabin giving us very little open floor space. We had boxes stacked around and under everything possible. Then we proceeded to find, cut and split firewood for the winter which turned out to be hardly enough for a few months.

It was about 1 ½ miles to the river from our cabin and we put the 55 gallon barrel in the back of our 48 Chevy pickup truck to haul water. Using the two buckets I would fill the barrel from the river. One of the washtubs would sit just inside the top of the barrel to keep the water from sloshing out all over the place on the drive back to the cabin.. I had a 15 gallon crock with a spigot on the side for keeping drinking water in the cabin which I would fill immediately with the cold river water. At that time we did not have to boil our drinking water, but in today's world I would not think of drinking water directly from a river without boiling it due to all the contaminants.

Our property was located about 50 miles from the nearest town. The last 27 miles of road was all gravel and dirt coming from the desert floor at about 2400 foot elevation up a steep 9 mile canyon to about 6000 foot elevation, then slowly climbing up over a 7500 foot pass before dropping down into the meadows where we lived at 6500 feet. There were only three families living on the mountain at that time. The first family was the McConnell's, with two young boys, at the top of the canyon about 10 miles off the highway, then we were another 15 miles inland and the last family was the Higham's, with three young boys, five miles beyond us at the Old Porter Ranch. All located in the high mountains but not close neighbors. We had to keep the snow plowed off the road in the winter time for the 27 miles to the highway without any outside help from the county. That was a big job and sometimes took all night long and then Dick had to go to work that day. All of us living up there loved the country and would not trade the winter hardships for a home in town. We were the only ones who had to commute for a job which was very challenging at times. Sometimes the snow drifts would get so bad that you could not find the roadway and Dick would not make it home but that was very seldom.

Some winters we would have an abundance of snow and our plowing of the road would leave a deep furrow to drive in with snow berms reaching over 6 feet tall on both sides of the road. So many nights we would drive for hours plowing the road but one night really sticks in our memory. We had a very unusual storm that dropped about 5 feet of snow overnight. When we tried to go plow we could hardly get out of our own driveway. So we proceeded to make our way over to the abandoned logging camp where some heavy equipment was stored for the next season of logging. At this time we had a few other families that had come up the mountain for the weekend and were now snowed in with us. The men worked at getting a large caterpillar tractor running and then Dick asked me to follow him with our four wheel drive car as he plowed the road open. The winds were blowing quite hard that night and the snow was drifting as fast as you could clear it so I was told to follow close behind Dick and not get stuck. Well, he was stopped by a big drift and proceeded to back up without my knowing it and I was almost run over by the caterpillar tractor! Dick came back to be sure I and our vehicle were both OK and then warned me to pay closer attention and not follow quite so close. I assured him the lesson was learned well on my part!

Many weekends we would go through a 55 gallon barrel of fuel while plowing the road along with our full truck tanks. This was a costly venture and we noticed that our neighbors would plan their trips to town for shopping on our schedule following us down the mountain and waiting to return behind us in the evening. So we decided to ask them for a bit of assistance with the plowing, like pitching in a few dollars for fuel and or taking turns riding with Dick while he plowed during the night. That turned out to be a real dud as only two people ever gave us any assistance. This was the price we paid for wanting to live in the wilderness while holding down a job in town, fifty miles away. It was not long before other people saw how we made living in the mountains possible and more people began to move up the mountain. Although it was several years before our little community really grew with year round residents. Most people just could not handle the hardships, as they called extra work involved with life off the grid.

We did not have any telephones, television or other communications for many years on the mountain. Then we put in CB radios which was nice in emergencies to communicate between neighbors and have in our vehicles. Eventually we ran lines on the ground and put in hand crank telephones between ranches, a new general store, Forest Service and BLM stations. We called our service the Johnson Ding-a-ling Phone Service and we had an antique switch board in our cabin. This phone system took time to lay out the lines and required annual maintenance on the lines as the ravens loved to chew off the insulation material. We would walk the lines and make any necessary repairs about once a year. Now you have some idea of where and how we were living.

Just imagine a young, just turned 19 year old with a new baby and only cloth diapers, along with her 23 year old husband leaving the big city for a life of adventure in the wilderness with no running water or electricity as the story begins in September 1962...............

Part One

Chapter 1

LEARNING TO LIVE ALONE

We are into the fall of 1962, all settled into our new little cabin and learning how to handle many new situations of life out here in the wilderness. It is such a pleasure to wake up in the crisp morning air and smell the lovely pine trees with the birds singing. You cannot appreciate true peace and silence until you have spent some time in the wilderness with only nature sounds. It is very rejuvenating to ones soul and allows you to get to know ones self to the very core. Often I turn on the radio just to hear voices and listen to mostly country music or an occasional talk show in the evening. We learned to cherish our radio novels like "The Green Hornet", "Inner Sanctum", "The Lone Ranger" and several others that were broadcast in the evenings. We could pick up radio stations from San Francisco (KGO), Denver (KOB) and Albuquerque (KOA) for various talk shows and news broadcasts. Then I always listened in the day time to KUZZ from Bakersfield for my favorite country music.

Dick had been job hunting daily, driving 100 miles round trip to town, but not having any luck. It seems that the town, Ridgecrest, California, is quite closed to strangers and we do not know anyone here for local references but we will make it work out for us. It is a bit discouraging to have Dick return home without any prospects for a paying job but we make each other laugh and challenge each other to some Cribbage games with best out of three games the winner of the evening. After four months of no job we decided to collect unemployment until spring when maybe a job would open up for us. So for the only time in our lives Dick accepted unemployment checks for the next four months until he found a job at a service station in town. That was quite a step down from his good electronics technician job he held at Lockheed Aircraft Corporation for the first year after we married. But we were very happy to be living where we chose and knew that one day things would get better for us.

I thought that it would be a bit scary to be alone for many hours without Dick around but that was not true. I was so busy just doing my household chores and laundry of diapers almost daily that I did not have time to even think about being alone with the baby. Life settled into a nice routine and still left me time for reading and some peaceful time with the country.

One of the first things I needed to learn was how to make bread for all the sandwiches that Dick ate daily. An old friend of ours from the city had given me her recipe and I proceeded to start practicing bread making. Well, the first two loaves came out just like building bricks and Dick said we could use them for the foundation under the cabin! That did not make me happy but I had to laugh with him at the horrible loaves. It seems that no one ever mentioned there is a big difference of cooking at sea level in Los Angeles and cooking at high altitude of 6500 feet. Since I did not own a cookbook it was many hours of trial and error before I learned how to cook many things but eventually my bread became well known for its high quality. Thank heavens for that redemption! I was even selling bread to a bachelor friend for a couple of years until he left the mountain. By this time I had learned to really enjoy baking all our pastries and cookies from "scratch" without all the instant boxes or frozen ready made items.

Learning to live without a refrigerator was a big challenge too. We kept a large ice chest under the cabin in the shade where it was quite cool, even without any ice, to hold our fresh foods which seemed to work most of the time. Only in mid-summer did we have problems due to the hotter outside temperatures and I would use block ice when I could get it. Then we reverted to mostly can goods and dry goods for our foods. As the children grew up we used powdered milk mixed with a can of evaporated milk (one can per gallon of powdered milk mixed up with water). This worked well and since they did not know any different they even liked it! Other drinks consisted of apple juice, Tang for orange juice, powdered lemonade mix but mostly just plain water. Then we used various Kool-aid mixes for a treat once in a while. Life was much simpler back then but we did not have any dental problems and our children were quite healthy. When in town doing our shopping it was a real treat to stop and have a soft drink or an ice cream cone.

Our first winter in the wilderness was quite a learning experience all the time. We were limited on our traveling around due to lack of funds. Dick did not find a job until late spring but we were alright as far as food for our baby and some canned and dry goods. As spring drew near we had run out of fresh meat and had no money so Dick went out one evening with his rifle and told me to start some potatoes. I laughed at him looking like a great hunter but shortly I heard a shot and he was soon back at the cabin with a nice rabbit already skinned. We were as happy as ever with fresh meat for dinner. He said the rabbit gave himself away looking up through a vee in a tree trunk making for a perfect shot without any meat ruined. That was the best rabbit we ever ate!

The biggest problem for me was I missed family and friends. It would get very lonely at times and we had no way to even communicate except by US mail. I became an avid letter writer and would mail off the many pages whenever I would get into town. Getting letters in return was like having Christmas but I soon found out that everyone was so busy with their own lives and their letters came very seldom. That is when I learned to make my own little world and family my priority for happiness. Sounds a bit harsh maybe but it worked out well for us and we had a wonderful, happy time without any outside interferences. It wasn't long before we realized that you know many people in your life but very few are real friends. We did manage to maintain a few very good friends even though we lived so far away. Our neighbors became our "family" and we shared with them all the good and bad family times. Our holidays were spent together as well. Our sons soon thought of Pauline and Jack Horton as grandparents because we shared so much of our time and holidays with them.

Learning to use a wood stove was quite a fight for me. It seems that the darn thing would always want to smoke indoors no matter what I did when starting the fire. We would let the fire burn out at night and by morning it was cold enough inside to freeze our dog's water in his dish. Since I was the first one up it was my job to get the home fires burning. This brought on some colorful language at times but I did get better as the months went by. I even learned to bake in a cast iron pot on top of the wood stove eventually. So the lesson learned was "never give up—perseverance wins"!! It was about this time that I read the book, "The Egg and I" which I could really relate too and it made me laugh until I cried!!

Living at the higher elevation of 6500 feet in the High Sierra Mountains was very different from sea level where I grew up. First of all it got COLD with temperatures down to -20 degrees sometimes and we had snow up to 5 feet deep. Our little cabin was not insulated which did not help us. I was not prepared for this at all. In fact we did not even own snow suits or boots. Dick always wore his western boots back then but we finally found some good insulated boots for him to wear to work. I wore lace shoes called Hush Puppies at the time. We each had a pair of knee high rubber boots we wore with two pair of wool socks when out in the snow. I was so glad we had our first winter alone together to overcome all the adversities and learn how to do various things for survival. By the second winter we were equipped with long john underwear, snow boots, good gloves, hats and coats. Our baby was prepared quite well with thermal knit sleepers and larger blanket sleepers to go over them which kept him very cozy.

One day we decided to try to help a couple of young Navy recruits that had gone off into Rock House Basin for the weekend when a snow storm hit stranding the two men. Dick and I along with our baby son took off in our pickup truck to rescue the two men. As we drove through the closed up Boy Scout Summer Camp we picked up our friend, Jim Hollingsworth, the scout ranch caretaker, who was ready to go on an adventure too. We had to travel several miles down a steep canyon on a two rutted trail, cross the south fork of the Kern River and then off through a burned area to get to the stranded men. We had almost reached the cabin where they were staying when we got really stuck. Our jack did not work at the time to get us out of trouble; it was getting colder and later in the evening, so we started to walk out 12 miles back to the nearest cabins at the Boy Scout Ranch which was closed for the winter. Everything was going well we thought but we were very tired and hungry. I had remembered to bring food for the baby but nothing for us! Jim was a much faster hiker than us with a baby so he went on ahead saying he would get his jeep and come back for us. When we reached the river crossing I felt that I could not go on without some rest and I lay down on my coat in the snow. Dick turned and saw me at which time he came over and yanked me up yelling, "You must walk and keep warm or you will freeze." With his encouragement and pushing me I did continue on and we waded across the river. Now we were wet to the knees, cold and tired but still we had several miles to a cabin where we could build a fire to warm up. After a few more miles we heard Jim coming in his jeep and what a glorious sound that was. That was not a good day but we survived and learned a lot about hypothermia first hand!! The next day Dick and Jim returned to get our truck and bring the two men out with them so the encounter ended quite well.

By spring a normal day would start at 5am with Dick getting ready for work, his first job was in a Union 76 service station in town at the minimum pay rate but we did not care. It was a job and we were taking care of ourselves living where we chose. People would eventually get to know Dick and his work ethics and he would move up in the job market, we were confident of this. Dick soon had a second part time job as a carpenter's helper working with a family owned building contractor in town. The skills learned here would benefit us for many years in our various adventures. I would pack him a nice lunch and thermos full of coffee while he ate breakfast before leaving about 5:30 to commute to town which was about 1 ½ hour drive one way. If the baby was still asleep I would go back to bed for a while to get some much needed rest too.

Then my day would be filled with our baby which everyone knows is a full time job plus doing laundry by hand in two wash tubs with a scrub board, getting firewood, hauling water from the river when needed, baking bread or other chores. I had purchased some books on self-teaching to knit, crochet and other useful crafts so I would practice a new craft until I had it down by making all our gloves, mittens, hats and sweaters along with blankets. I learned to sew and made shirts for our family along with other items using a treadle sewing machine. I even tried candle making but found it was much cheaper to just purchase the few candles we ever used. Life for me was like stepping back into the last century but was very satisfying as I learned to do so many things the old way. One can not find words to express the great feeling you have inside when you have done something totally self sufficient without using modern tools or power. Seeing the beginning and working through to the end of a project producing something you really need is very satisfying indeed. I believe too many of our young people today have never had this satisfaction in life nor the anticipation of waiting until you can afford to purchase a particular item needed.

Our only lights were regular kerosene wick lamps and these had to be filled daily, twice a day in the middle of winter, plus washing the glass globes about twice a week. When our son was napping I would spend some time outdoors cutting small branches into firewood with my bow saw, which I stacked right outside the door against the cabin front. I called this squaw wood because it did not require a lot of heavy sawing like big trees. The big trees were cut up together with Dick using his grandfather's six foot long two-man hand saw. In fact we cut all our firewood for many years with that old saw. Dick and I never owned a chain saw until after we moved to Alaska more than 18 years later.

One project for me to make things feel like a home was to find and line the edges of our circle driveway with rocks and to make a couple of rock flower gardens. I would use our dishwater on the flower beds to make the flowers grow and add color to our yard. I was very proud of my little colorful yard. One day Dick came home and said that I needed to stop watering with the dish water as it would draw wild animals into the yard. We had deer, bear, coyotes, mountain lions and more. I was convinced to use only gray water, bath water and laundry water, from that time on.

So we proceeded to dig a large hole about 6x6x6 feet, on the other side of the yard, and cover it over with a plywood platform that had a trap door in it where I would empty our "honey bucket pot" and dish water from. This honey bucket pot, a bucket type toilet, was kept indoors and emptied daily out in the hole in the ground in place of the outhouse. Dick built a small box with a toilet seat and lid that sat over the bucket making it look neat in the corner of the cabin. That was so very nice to not have to go outside all the time. I learned to use a bit of water and plain bleach in the pot which kept the odors away. Using that honey bucket for more than six years felt very modern because it was inside our living quarters. I felt spoiled especially when it was freezing cold outside.

Over the next few months Dick held several jobs. He had to quit the service station job after less than two months because it did not pay enough to cover our fuel bills for the truck commute to town. We were going backwards financially. Our goal was to get a job with the Forest Service where we could still live in the mountains and not have to commute for paychecks. Dick was hired by the Forest Service but it was a part time position as an emergency fire fighter and camp ground maintenance man. This was hard work as there were only two men to cover a large area with several campgrounds and many miles of trails but the pay was good and he had a foot in the door so to speak for a permanent position, we hoped. Well, sometimes our hopes are met in different ways and this was one of those times. About the time the Forest Service was ready to cut back for the winter Dick found a job with a logging company that was going to work as far into the winter as possible before the snow stopped them. So Dick began as a choker setter and did a lot of other labor positions as well. The pay was greater than the part time forest service job and we were feeling good because we would be financially set for the winter season. Each time we went to town together Dick would still check in with applications filed at the Navy Base for an electronics position and we would wait and wait.....

Dick always loved being an electronics technician but there was not much chance of that in Kennedy Meadows until we had a letter from China Lake Naval Weapons Center down in the local desert with an offer of a job. Dick was to start work just before Christmas 1963 as a laborer until the apprentice program opened the next summer. It was about this time we learned we were going to have a second baby which was not a surprise as we had planned to have them about two years apart. We hoped they would be playmates and friends growing up. Dick worked doing hard labor running jack hammers and such until he entered the electronics apprentice program in August 1964. We were so excited for him to finally reach his dream of working in the electronics field once again even though it meant starting at the bottom as an apprentice. Dick would be going to college a few nights per week over the next four years while working an 8 hour per day shift, Monday through Friday, at the Naval Weapons Center doing research and development of weapons systems. He was so excited and we soon learned how to live with his very busy schedule which left almost no time for family. We made a pact to always spend Sunday afternoons together and take picnic lunches to the river to play since we would hardly see one another during the rest of the week. Dick left home at 5:30am and was home by 6pm when he did not have classes, then it was 11pm or later depending on the weather. The early nights at home were spent doing homework for school classes and homework every Saturday all day long. This was very hard for a young newly married couple with a small baby and toddler. I felt like a single parent at times as I did not have any help whatsoever with the children. Many times I had to work at keeping the boys quiet for daddy to study by taking them outdoors a lot and putting them to bed early when Dick was home. This schedule persisted for the next four years. During the summers he was not in school and we would take camping trips on a weekend now and then. That was the only type of vacation we could afford but we loved it and the many different places we could explore right around in the mountains where we lived and also down in the desert area around the town.

Dick and I were getting tired of hauling all our water and decided we needed to put in a well. After checking out all the local drilling companies we decided we did not have the funds for that so we would just hand dig a well ourselves. After all how hard can that be?? Using pick and shovels we started in digging and found that we had to get some lumber to shore up the sides as we went down to keep the ground from caving in on us. So we proceeded to dig a 5 foot by 3 foot well (room enough to swing a pick and shovel), build and install shoring and repeat this pattern until we reached about 16 feet down and ran into very hard blue granite. This would require drilling and dynamite to go further. Dick had learned a little about dynamite when working for the logging company building road spurs so he joined one of the miners for a few days for more instructions and we entered into the next phase of well drilling. We bought a diamond drill bit with a three foot shaft and using a 15 pound sledge hammer we hand drilled our holes with me holding the bit and slowly turning it as Dick pounded it down giving us a two foot hole about 1 ½ inch diameter. This would take us two days to complete one hole for dynamite. We would put in at least two holes each time. This was a very slow process and we did not complete this well for two years but we continued to work on it every chance we had.

One day a neighbor, Carl Austin, came by to see how we were getting along with the dynamite program and he was amazed at our drilling process which had taken us down to about the 21 foot level so far. Carl soon returned with his old air compressor and jack hammer for us to use for drilling our holes. That equipment made the digging go so much faster. Soon we were moving at a rate of two feet down a weekend. The noise of the air compressor was terrible but we put up with it just to get ahead on the digging. Our dog would lay in the shade of the air compressor watching over our two boys while we worked at mucking out the hole in the ground. Then one day we had a bit of a mishap and learned how fast one can train a dog!! After Dick would set the dynamite and connect the wiring for the electric caps to set it off he would quickly climb out of the hole and say, "Ready?" At this point I would untwist my end of the electrical wires and connect them to the truck battery to set off the dynamite which would blow and send some dust and rock into the air. This process worked very well until one day when I was getting tired and I slid across the truck seat to put the wires to the battery and the static electricity created by my rear end sliding across the seat set off the blast prematurely. This shocked both me and Dick but the dog was really struck as he jumped up so hard and fast he almost knocked himself out on the bottom of the air compressor before taking off running to hide. After that anytime Dick would say "ready" our dog would go on a fast run away from the windmill area which brought great laughter from all of us watching him.,

Dick constructed a wooden frame work with 2x4's to fit over our well hole with a wooden windlass to turn by hand and wind up the rope carrying the buckets of rubble to the top for disposal. After setting off our dynamite and allowing at least one hour for the hole to clear the bad air by a canvas funnel we made to hang down into the hole, one of us would climb down a ladder to fill the buckets at the bottom of the well while the other pulled the buckets up to dump them on our pile. We took turns at the jobs to keep things from getting boring. The person up on the ground level was responsible for keeping an eye on our boys to keep them from getting hurt as they played on the piles of rubble. Actually one of the boys was still in a playpen during the first year making it much easier. After two years we had finally gone as far as we wanted to and had good water but not a large supply, about 50 gallons a day. On Dick's last day of drilling with the jack hammer he started feeling creepy like the walls were coming in on him as we had actually blasted out a very large hole near the bottom at 44 feet. When I was down mucking out the debris I began to have the same feeling so we decided to quit right there and seal it off for our well. We had been working in water for about 20 feet by then. It was so exciting to see the water creeping in through the clay gapes in the rock walls. We also learned that it is really cold down in a well even on a very hot day outdoors, hence the saying "it was colder than a well diggers a--!" So very true too.

One of our new friends came over to check on our progress regularly while digging the well and asked us just how we planned on getting the water out of the well eventually. We really wanted to put up a windmill but have not looked into the prices yet. This man then made us an offer we could not refuse. He had a windmill that had stood in downtown Manhattan Beach, California for more than a century, over on his ranch which was missing some parts. When the city took the windmill down he bought it and never got around to actually putting it together again. It was in a pile of pieces and we could have it for one dollar. Well, we jumped at the chance and when Dick opened his wallet he did not even have a one dollar bill inside so the man loaned us the money which we paid back the following week. That was so great to have just what we needed to make running water on OUR LAND. The next week we drove over to pick up all the pieces and bring it home. I asked Dick if he knew how to put it together and he said, "No, but you and I are going to learn how!" Then I wanted to know about the missing pieces and Dick replied, "Whatever we don't have we will make ourselves. After all it is only just a bunch of steel pieces." I loved his spunk and knowing that we could do this no matter what happens. Well, that turned out to be quite a project that took several weeks and a fire with anvil to make parts needed but we did accomplish the completion of the windmill. We had poured a cement foundation for the tower and placed angle iron legs in the cement to hook the windmill legs to. Now it was time to stand up this 30 foot three legged tower with a 150 pound gear box on the top. We used our pickup truck as sort of a dead man putting an old hand winch inside the cab and running a cable out the open back window to hook the cable to the top of the tower which was lying on the ground. Dick would hand winch the tower up until the front end of the truck came off the ground at which time I would raise the tower using long 2x6 lumber to hold it off the ground and let the truck front end return to ground level. We repeated this process over and over using longer 2x6 boards each time until we had enough of an angle to raise the tower all the way up. I was using a rope to stop the tower from going over too far. As soon as we had all three legs bolted to the cemented legs we celebrated. The hardest part of the job was done and we were both still alive and well!!! Then we started the installation of the windmill blades that created a ten foot diameter fan connected to the geared motor on the top of the tower. Dick looked so small up there trying to connect each set of three blades, for a total of about 18 blades, as we hoped for the weather to remain calm. The first time we turned on the motor to see if the blades were balanced correctly you could hear us singing for miles around!!! Eventually we finished the plumbing of the well head and turned on the blades to pump the first water on July 31, 1966, almost four years after moving up on the mountain. We were so happy that we proceeded to have a water fight with our boys' right there in the front yard. Dick even took some old 8mm movie film of all this going on. Such joy over a simple thing as water on our land!

Learning to use dynamite was fun but very disappointing to me. My only experience was seeing this in movies where the bad guys would toss a stick of dynamite onto the mountain side and the whole thing blew up closing the pass. The first time we set some dynamite off I was so shocked to hear only a small bloop and very little dust fly. Dick said that was good because it meant the dynamite did its job. I never believed movies again! We had to dynamite the foundation holes for our new house pillars into blue granite on the top of the little knoll right in the middle of our land. We started to build our own home in the summer of 1965 doing a little at a time as we had the money. We started with buying a few sacks of concrete and some concrete blocks and rebar each payday and would try to purchase a bit of lumber each payday. It did not take long before we had a building up with a roof on it. Our home was a simple ranch style three bedroom, two bathrooms, living room open to dining/kitchen room. It was not a huge place, 1144 square feet, but very nice and roomy for us.

I could not wait to get moved in to larger quarters, so I convinced Dick that we should get our furniture out of storage in town and bring it up the mountain to the house, saving the monthly rental for the storage. This would give us more money to work on finishing the house each month. So we brought all our belongings up the mountain even though we did not have windows or doors on the house yet. Dick put in a three old windows in some of our window holes and we boarded over the back door. The other window holes were tar papered over for the winter to keep the weather out. Then one day when he came home from work I met him in the driveway to let him know the boys and I had moved up the hill into the house. I had dinner ready and was carrying it up the hill to serve in our new home. Dick thought I was crazy to make more work for myself like this but we sure loved having so much more room indoors. It was not long before we had the propane hooked up to the house and the cook stove from the cabin moved along with the propane refrigerator that we had purchased. Wow, we were living in real fashion now with room to dance around inside!! What a grand party we had that evening! I guess you could say it never takes much to give us a lot of happiness in life.

We soon decided to break down the old A-frame cabin and use it for firewood to clear out our front yard. By this time it was completely empty and we thought it could be knocked down so easy by backing our truck into it and pushing it over. So Dick took a good run at it and it never budged so we tried again and again before giving up and using hammers and saws to tear it down. That fall it kept us warm for the last time as it burned in our wood stove in the house!

About this time in our lives I felt that I had to do more than just stay home with two babies so I started to volunteer at the small one room school that had started up for the logging families that were staying on the mountain about eight miles above us. I was able to bring my boys along with me and they enjoyed the other children but this did not last long. When the first good snow storm hit most of the families left the mountain and shortly thereafter the school closed. Then I had the opportunity to work at the local general store that had opened about the time we moved up the mountain. I started out part time and moved up to full time running the store alone during the weekdays which lasted until both our sons were in school. (Our sons attended school down the mountain in town because we felt it was very important for them to have the socializing with other youngsters and get the best education we could provide.) The owners of the store would come up for the weekends and I stayed home except during the big three holiday weekends of summer when we all worked trying to keep the place going. Yes, it was a very busy area for family camping vacations, fishing and hunting. These times were always such fun as we each had our children with us at work too. Saturday nights we would show old time movies outdoors on a big screen just off the store parking lot. Many of the campers came to enjoy some old time western movies in the wilderness theater, including popcorn from an old wagon. We had so much good old fashioned fun back then and it did not cost much for a family.

Chapter 2

HAVING A REGULAR SCHEDULE

By the time Dick finished his four years of college and graduated from the electronics apprentice program in 1968 with the Outstanding Apprentice Award and highest grade point average we were settled into a good life up on the mountain. When he was presented with the award plaque along with a $250.00 check I was so excited that I blurted out, "Wow, now we can get a flush toilet!" When everyone around me began to laugh I realized I had said this out loud and I was so embarrassed that I could have crawled under the table to hide. This was a big deal to us! We used that check for our construction and had the plumbing all completed by September that year.

The previous year we worked on hand digging the septic tank hole for a 1500 gallon two compartment cement tank to be installed. That is a lot of pick and shovel work for two people. Then we hand dug all the 75 foot long leach line ditches that were three foot wide by three foot deep. The gravel for the leach line was all hand picked from the riverbed during the weekends as we let the boys play in the water for a while. We would fill up the trunk of our VW bug and then empty the rocks into the ditch when we got home. It was a slow process but it was free and that we liked!! Besides it gave us some good exercise bending over. It seemed like very little time before we were ready to go purchase our bathroom fixtures and finally have a tub/shower, flushing toilets and sinks. Dick's mother was visiting us on Labor Day Weekend in September 1968 when we had the plumbing all finished and were flushing the toilet for the first time. It was so much fun as we all gathered into the bathroom to watch the water flow through the toilet the first time. You never heard such laughter and howling at our fabulous progress!! Only six years and two children after moving from the big city, and here we are with hot and cold water running into and out of the house automatic without our help and flush toilets! We were all so very happy. The next day we had a celebration of burying the "honey bucket" since we no longer needed it. The honey bucket was our sort of porta-potty that we took outdoors to empty into a large hole in the ground.

We planned to place a 1000 gallon water tank on a steel tower out behind our house where we would have good gravity feed and we built a small building, matching our house, over the water tank with insulation. The pipeline into the house would run in an insulated box from the tank to our attic where the house insulation would be over the top of the pipeline. This would allow the house heat to keep the water from freezing in the winter time as all pipes would be running inside the ceiling with a lot of insulation over the top. This system worked so well for us that we were the only house for many years to have running water year round on the mountain. Our well pump line to the water tank was automatically drained back into the well after filling the tank each week by using a check valve right at the water tank. This left the main line dry except when pumping.

Now the funny thing about this fifteen foot tall steel tower holding the water tank and small cover building was that it stood on an uneven hill behind our house. So when we went to purchase the 4 inch angle iron to make the legs for the tower each leg was a different length. We had them precut at the steel yard and the men working there took bets that we would never have a level platform for the water tank. But they did not know my husband who could plan, draw out and precisely construct what he wanted! Our tower which was over braced between each leg turned out perfectly and we rolled the new tank into place using ropes on a plane of long lumber. We were very proud of this accomplishment especially when we continued to have running water year round.

The first time I filled up the bathtub with warm water including a lot of bubble bath in it for the boys to share in some fun I was shocked to find they did not want to get in the tub. Both boys were crying saying it was to deep and too much water for a bath. We finally talked them into at least trying it out and they had bubbles all over the bathroom that night! I never heard so much fun squealing and laughter over bath time as we had that night. These are the memories that last a life time. I just loved not having to pick up the heavy galvanized tub and carry it out the back door to empty it after bath time. We never had any arguments at bath time again!

By this time we had purchased a new wringer washing machine from Sears in April 1966 to do our laundry, AFTER OUR YEARS of diapers. I would run a generator once a week for a few hours to clean our clothes. Talk about getting modern, we were living grand now! Dick taught me to weld and I made my first set of clothes line poles out of 1 ½ inch galvanized pipe. Then after digging holes for the poles I cemented them in the ground about 15 feet apart and strung 6 cable lines for my clothes drying. My lines were on eye bolts with small turn buckles so I could keep them tight as they stretched out over the years. There is nothing like the wonderful smell of fresh air dried laundry without all the chemical softeners used today.

By this time we had installed our windows and doors in the house and hand built pegged knotty pine kitchen cupboards. Our home was really beginning to look great and we had managed this all by ourselves without the use of power tools for the most part or going into debt. It was so fabulous to know we did it ourselves by just using "how to do" books for direction on the various types of construction including electrical and plumbing. We had even visited the county building department and picked up all the codes and regulations so we would build to meet all the requirements. Many people have said we should have just bought a house but we would say, "Why, we own this one outright and you have a mortgage for many years?" Besides we have both learned so very much along the way as we worked at it together.

In 1967 Dick decided we could build a home power system using nine 12 volt car batteries connected in series to give us a house supply at 120 volts DC. This system was very similar to the old fashion Delco system used on farms in the Midwest back in the 1930's. We were pretty excited about having some real electricity for our home. We had a big laugh after our visit to the local catalog order shop for Sears in town when we ordered nine of their biggest amperage car batteries. The man asked if we wanted the best warrantee for them and Dick said NO because you won't cover them anyway. When we were asked why we thought that Dick explained just what we planned to use the batteries for. The man was incredulous! Then we remembered we needed another battery for a vehicle at home and asked if we could get a discount purchasing ten batteries at one time. To our surprise the store gave us a very good discount and we laughed all the way home. Our new batteries would arrive in two weeks.

Dick designed and built a direct type charger for the batteries, using four diodes mounted in a block of cooling fins, so we could directly charge them once a week when running a generator. To start out we were using an old Rambler engine and alternator to charge batteries. Then Dick's parents visited us and were so impressed with our progress that they bought us a Briggs and Stratton 5hp engine that Christmas, to belt-drive our alternator. We had a small dynamotor, military surplus, to convert our power to AC to run a vacuum sweeper, our record player and other household items. Every Saturday morning we would run the generator for a couple of hours to charge batteries and do our laundry. This routine seemed to work out great for our needs. Having real electricity in the house was such a pleasure and we began living just like other people down in town.

Dick did modify some of my kitchen appliances so I could use them directly off the DC power which did not require the use of the inverter running. We had added in line switches that were instant acting on my electric mixer and toaster. These switches were placed right in the electric cord and still exist there today. DC power needs to have instant on/off switching or the points in a switch will arc and melt together. So after having the switch points melt on my appliances Dick fixed them with the in-line switches and I never had a problem with them again.

In today's world we would be called living very green back in the 1960's, but we just felt it was economical. Of course we learned to be very aware of all power usage in our home. Water was never wasted or left running unnecessarily. Lights were never left on if no one was using it immediately. We also still used mostly kerosene lamps for our lights just because we liked the ambiance of them. By this time we had discovered the old Aladdin lamps that used a wick and mantle which gave off a lot of light for reading. The Aladdin lamps produced the lighting of about a 75 watt bulb. We purchased several of these tall brass lamps for our main living quarters and one hung over the dining room table. We needed to have extra tall chimneys because of our high altitude and also put big screens on the top of the chimneys to preserve our mantles much longer, just like in a Coleman lantern the cloth mantle falls apart when a flying insect touches it. We still have quite a supply of the various lamp parts, extra mantles and chimneys since we have always lived out in the wilderness where stores are non-existent. Our regular old wick kerosene lamps from the cabin were used in our bedrooms in the house.

Many people were very concerned that we had all these kerosene lamps about with small children but our sons have known only these types of lamps during their growing up years and are very careful around them. They know how to light them and trim the wicks too. We went for many years without any accidents with kerosene lamps from 1962. Then in 1993 during a holiday visit with our sons and grandchildren visiting us, our sons and Dick got into a wrestling match and overturned a burning lamp off the table between our two recliner chairs spilling kerosene all over the stuffed chair. Dick instantly reached for the fallen lamp to blow out the flame while the boys, now grown men, ran for towels to mop up the kerosene. Of course my beautiful hand painted glass shade was in pieces on the floor and the cabin was so quiet you could hear a pin drop. I was shocked at the mess and so surprised to see there was not a fire at all but my fury with the three men was pegged at maximum! When I turned back to my work in the kitchen without saying a word I heard one of the boys say, "Wow, we are really in trouble now, Mom didn't even say a word!!" After I calmed down I informed them they owe me a new lamp shade and I want one exactly like the one I had, also if you ever wrestle in my house again you will be dead meat!!! That lamp shade cost $350.00 and came from Tennessee. The lamp shade was replaced and only a week later I accidentally dropped it breaking it in pieces making me cry. When I called for another replacement the woman asked what happened this time and we both laughed after I told my story.

Our home was totally self-sufficient as we produced our own water using a windmill, we made our own electricity and we had installed two 500 gallon propane tanks which we had filled once a year. By this time we had purchased a second Servel propane single door refrigerator which we used as a freezer, by removing all the cowling around the freezer compartment and keeping it turned as cold as it would go. We had a propane 40 gallon water heater. We had installed two propane wall heaters that used outside air to burn, one for the living area and one for the bedroom area set at a lower temperature. These were very efficient heaters and much more healthy. Since we were gone all day every day this kept our home warm. We burned wood in our free standing fireplace when we were home to cut down on the propane usage. Our cost of living remained much lower than any house in town and we loved that.

We had started out with one 500 gallon propane tank for our house but then one year we had a problem with the company filling the tank. The company would not come up the mountain unless they had enough calls to empty a full truck load as it took a full day to make the trip. I would ask them to come fill our tank during the summer when usage was quite low by everyone and then we would have it topped off once again sometime during the spring on one of their trips up the mountain to fill propane tanks. Anyway, I asked them to come fill us one year and each time they came up the mountain other residents or businesses seemed to empty their truck before they reached us. Then the snow started falling and we stopped to ask them once again to fill us and they refused to come for one customer only. Dick informed them that we had been a long standing customer and have asked repeatedly for a filling but were passed over during each of the recent trips up the mountain. So now we are almost totally empty and we are going to get propane with either you or us driving that truck up the mountain before the snow gets to bad. So we are asking now, what time do you want to leave here today? Our tanks were filled that afternoon. We asked what is the minimum delivery they would make, which was 1000 gallons of propane, so we installed a second tank and had them filled once a year in the middle of summer. They never had an excuse again to not keep us filled up. One benefit of this summer filling plan was that propane was at the cheapest rate during the summer months of low usage.

Our life became very scheduled as we commuted to work for us and school for the boys daily. Leaving the house at 6am and returning by 6pm. Saturdays the boys and Dick did the various outdoor chores while I did our laundry, cleaned house and baked bread and cookies. Sundays were more or less family play days which were never really planned but just sort of happened.

CHAPTER 3

FAMILY PLAYING TOGETHER

As we entered the winter season of 1968/69 we felt much more comfortable about taking time to get out and enjoy life a bit instead of always working away from home or on our home. The house was not finished yet but was all closed in with some of the inside walls done. We now had good indoor plumbing, heating and electrical. Plus Dick's wages had increased after finishing his apprentice program which gave us a bit more money to play with our sons. It was at this time during one of our exploration trips by four wheel drive that we discovered some great places across the Mojave Desert to go camping. We made an agreement to take one weekend a month from here on out to take our boys and go off on a camping trip. These trips would be planned together with our family so everyone had some input on the adventures.

Sometimes we would go backpacking on one of the many trails in the High Sierras within a few miles of our home. That was always fun as we had started the boys backpacking at ages 3 and 5 with their own tiny aluminum pack frames that would carry their own sleeping bag and jacket. To keep them hiking without complaint we had an incentive program of pieces of penny candy awarded after ever two miles. Then we would always stop by a creek for lunch so the boys could play in the water for a while as I prepared our meal. Catching and having fresh golden trout on these trips was always a special treat as well. The boys seemed to really enjoy these trips and always looked forward to the next one. We would hike up and over passes at 10,000 feet or more and down canyons looking for Indian relics which we sometimes found. Our dog, a black Labrador retriever, was a great companion along the trails as well and kept the boys busy following him. The dog carried his own food too.

Thinking back a ways, I remember my first hike with Dick after moving up on the mountain when our only son at the time was about six months old. We did not have one of those fancy Gerry packs for babies but Dick had an old wooden frame pack that we attached our baby car seat over to carry Robert. These car seats were made of an aluminum frame work with large hooks that would hang over the back of the front automobile seat and had a canvas seat for the baby to put his legs through, nothing like today's ergonomically safety minded baby seats. Anyway, I loved it as it gave me more freedom to drive with a baby on my own. By attaching this baby seat to the pack frame we could take hikes much more comfortably. Dick walked in front and I followed behind him with the baby looking toward me while hanging off Dick's back. We would sing songs and make silly antics to keep our baby laughing and having fun along with us. Then one day as we had to cross a deep ravine balancing along the top of a fallen log, I was waiting for Dick with the baby on the pack frame to get across before I started across. Suddenly the baby car seat canvas bottom broke loose and our son was dangling from the seat hanging on for dear life to the aluminum framework. I yelled to Dick and started running across the log to catch our son before he would fall many feet into the ravine. What a tight grip that little boy had! As I held on to little Robert he just laughed like this was all a great game but Dick and I gained many gray hairs that day!! We finished that hike with the baby being carried in our arms which gets very tiring after a few miles. After that Dick reinforced the whole seat affair with cable so it could not break again.

We had purchased our very first four wheel drive in February of 1968 after that extreme snow storm that hit us on the mountain. We had a nice International Scout and had plans to one day get a snow plow for the front end of the vehicle. Sometimes we would have friends and neighbors that would go along with us on a four wheel drive explorations in the desert. There were so many tracks open to the public back then that lead to old mining claims, Indian camps and other geological sites like remote hot springs. We saw many areas of pictographs and petroglyphs left by the Indians.

It was interesting to see how the natives had traded with the other tribes for items needed. Such as the mountain Indians traded pine nuts for obsidian glass for their arrowheads from the desert Indians. Our sons even learned to chip arrowheads from obsidian to make necklaces for us. For many years we would collect obsidian, a lovely black glass formed from erupting volcanoes, around the local area.

We found many huge rock areas that had grinding bowls in them where we assumed the pine nuts were ground by the Indians. So one year we decided we would learn what it was like to be gathering pine nuts to make bread. We had been collecting pine nuts every year and roasting them or eating them raw. Anyway, one year we collected nuts, roasted them in our fireplace and then ground then into flour to make two loaves of bread. This was a several day project requiring a lot of hand labor that we only did one time. No wonder the natives never had time for anything else beside hunting and gathering! Our sons would even bag the nuts by a handful into small paper bags and sell them to tourist for 25 cents to get extra spending money. We would laugh at people paying the boys for the nuts they would walk over but not pick up!! This was our children's great idea for raising funds for whatever was on their list of wanted item. After all it was hard to have a lemonade stand in the wilderness.

One of our four wheel trips found us exploring sand dunes in the various desert valleys. We had camped in Death Valley and were running around on the many trails from there. Eventually we wound up in Eureka Valley along the sand dunes which are among the highest dunes in the western states. Well, temptation won out and we had to try to drive the dunes like everyone else. There were tracks all over the place and Dick always like to make his own tracks so we would drive where others had not been. That proved to be a mistake this time as we went over a dune between two sets of tracks and came to a straight down drop off of about 12 feet. Of course we were flying pretty fast and went out quite a ways before going down, as our front end hit the hard pack ground Dick gave the throttle a boost so we pulled out flat instead of rolling end over end. The poor dog was doing his best to stay off of the gear shift and transfer case levers during the fall and was not happy with Dick about the abrupt landing either! By now we were into evening and decided it was best not to camp that night but drive out the 90 miles or so to a highway and head home while it was cool. We were pretty sure that we had severely damaged something under the vehicle and did not want it to fall apart this far from civilization. We did make it out and home just fine but had lost all confidence in our four wheel drive. So on Monday morning we drove the car into town to the dealer and wanted to trade it in on a new model. The dealer asked us why we wanted to trade a basically new car, less than a year old, and we said we liked what the new model offered more. The dealer took it for a test drive and gave us a great trade in and we drove home in a new Scout. Now that is not the end of the story. A few weeks later Dick had a phone call at work from a man that had purchased our old Scout and he asked just what had happened to that car. Dick asked him why? The man said he found the cast iron bell housing was cracked in two places and the floor pans were spider cracked all over along with two major cracks in the framework. We had no idea there were that many problems as we didn't even check to find out before trading the car in immediately. We were so lucky to even get that vehicle to town without a mishap. Dick told the man we were surprised as we had only jumped off a sand dune!

During these exciting camping trips we met many like minded families with children and soon developed a group of about 60 or more people that we would meet up with regularly at our favorite hot springs in the desert. Over the years we spent many weekends and spring vacations with various family groups and soon became like one huge family together. We still get together as often as possible but after all these years our group has slowly decreased due to aging and deaths. Now many of us meet up in the winters down in Arizona but we are all using RV's now instead of tent camping. Oh how the times have changed!

We managed over the years to take our boys to the big city down in Los Angeles County so they could see what that lifestyle was like. It was such fun watching them learn about elevators, escalators and lots of traffic and people everywhere. They were shocked that you could get on an elevator and come out in a different room altogether. They also liked to try to climb up the down escalators just because it was fun. We would drive down to have Thanksgiving holiday weekend with Dick's mother and then go do our Christmas shopping that Friday, all in one day. That was a real challenge to be able to complete everything in one day and get it all home without the boys seeing anything or knowing what we bought.

Thinking of shopping I should mention my normal shopping trips. I always kept a running list of groceries and other items needed because I only shopped twice a month. It was a 100 mile round trip to go shopping so you did not run to the store unnecessarily. We always carried an ice chest to get our cold stuff home without spoiling. To make our time count, we would plan to shop on a Thursday evening before our weekend a month getaway camping trip. I would take our laundry to town with us that day so after work we would stop at the Laundromat and load the machines with our laundry then leave the boys there to transfer the finished laundry into the dryers. The boys could work on their school homework while they waited. Dick and I would go to the market in the same parking lot and do all the grocery shopping. Then back to the laundry just in time for all four of us to fold the clothes and clean linens to take home. Following this we had a big treat of dinner with a milk shake at MacDonald's next door to the shopping plaza before heading up the mountain. With everyone working together we got all the major chores done and were free to go play over the weekend. This process worked out very well for us over the school years.

As our sons grew older we tried to give them many experiences in the big city once in a while as we took them to the big Barnum and Bailey Circus in Anaheim; Disneyland and Knott's Berry Farm another time; Six Flags Magic Mountain a couple of times; and various museums. The boys loved going to the beach along the west coast near Santa Barbara and playing in the surf and sand. Our oldest son said they should have named the ocean pepper water because it tasted so bad! This statement gave us many laughs over the years. We visited a few drive in theaters to see the latest Disney movies and most of John Wayne's westerns. One weekend we drove all the way to Lancaster, California, about 100 miles one way with our neighbors Jack and Pauline just to watch a new movie, John Wayne in the Cowboys. It was a spur of the moment decision and we loaded up and took off, stopping to pick up some hamburgers for dinner in the car as we arrived at the theater just as the movie was starting. We had a great time and did not get home until well after midnight.

One summer some friends with sons the same age as our boys asked if we would let our sons come to their home in Camarillo, California for a week stay. We were not to sure about letting our sons be away from home that long but felt assured that the supervision would be good and agreed to let them go. The boys had a most wonderful time and learned so much about city living from the other children but some of the things they learned we were not happy about, like reckless bicycling in city traffic, when Jeffrey was almost run over by a car because he did not look around properly. The other thing was learning how to sneak into a walk-in movie theater and watch two shows without paying! I was shocked at this news and not happy about that lesson at all. This was only the second time our boys had been away from home without us and the first time in a city environment, what an education it became!

The first time our boys were away from home without us they had been invited to spend a week during summer vacation with friends at Taboose Creek Ranch near Bishop, California. The boys were about 10 and 12 years of age at the time. Our friends had an old house trailer in their back yard and made it up like a guest cabin for the boys. Billie had put a bunch of store bought cookies, chips and snacks plus a small refrigerator with a case of soda pop in the trailer for the boys. Our sons were so surprised to have access to all of this that they really ate a lot during their evenings in the trailer alone. They had a television in the trailer and could watch as much television as they wanted. The creek ran right through the yard so fishing was easy which both boys enjoyed daily as well as picking delicious items from the garden and orchard. Billie said all they wanted to eat was fish and corn on the cob every day so she made them limit the meals of fish and corn, thankfully. Billie was so good with our boys teaching them many handcrafts during that week. Bob, Billie's husband, would take the boys out exploring in his old jeep and was amazed that the boys wanted to hurry and get back to the house as they had some television show they wanted to watch. This was all so amusing to us because no one had ever seen two children that were so in love with watching television over going exploring right then. But television was not available to our children at home so it was a big treat for them to watch and with unlimited access. This was the early 1970's and our sons were having a grand time.

CHAPTER 4
WINTER STORMS

Often we are asked if we ever have problems with major storms living out away from town so far. Well, as you may expect the answer is YES. But we do not let that keep us from having a great life, living where we choose to be. I can not even count the number of nights that we were so exhausted from staying up most of the night to plow the road 27 miles to the highway. Often I slept at home with the boys and Dick did the plowing all alone. I think all of this was much harder on my mother than it was on us because we knew what we were doing and she did not which scared the heck out of her.

Back in March of 1963 we had kidnapped my mother from a very abusive relationship and taken her up the mountain to live with us for one month to see if she wanted to start life over again. After that month Mom decided to start looking for a job down in town and stay near us. This made us very happy for her and she soon had a job working for the local phone company as a telephone operator. We had introduced Mom to our local deputy sheriff, a man closer to her age, who was divorced and a very good friend of ours. Those two hit it off immediately and became very close friends. Les would come by our cabin for coffee every day and challenge me to a couple of games of cribbage then play with our baby for a bit before finishing up his surveillance of the mountain cabins and businesses. Soon Les and Mom began to take picnics to the river together. When Mom moved to town because of her new job it was not long before Les followed her. It was very comical a few years later when they decided to get married that our boys were telling everyone in town that Grandma and Grandpa are getting married this weekend in the park. This brought many smiles from everyone seeing the blissful innocence of children.

Many times when we were in town we would stop to visit Mom and Les in the evening or the boys would go over to visit Grandpa Les after school for a while. This was so wonderful to have time to build a great relationship with both of them. Also, whenever Dick could not get home he always had a place to bed down on the sofa for the night but hardly ever did so. He remembers one night when he had to return to town due to heavy snowfall and my mother was so upset that I would not know where he was. We had a terrible time convincing Mom that Dick and I had an agreement to never venture out looking for the other one putting all of us in jeopardy at the time. Instead, if he could not make it home he just returned to town to try again the next day. I would wait up until 10pm and then go to bed knowing he would do the best he could to take care of himself for us. Yes, I did get some sleep so I could be together for the boys during the next day. Then we would watch out the window to look for daddy's truck as they would be the only headlights coming. It was always such a thrill to see those lights appear about three miles away as they came out of the woods into the open meadow and we knew daddy would be home soon. I was very thankful that this happened seldom and as everyone on the mountain would agree, you could set your clock by Dick's appearance each evening at 6pm.

Some people claimed that Dick led a charmed life because he always seemed to get through the really bad weather but that was not true. One morning after some very heavy rain all night he mentioned that he may not be able to return tonight but don't worry. I agreed and gave him a special big kiss and hug. After he left the skies opened up and we had about four inches of rain in only a few hours, then the flash floods starting flowing. Since our house was up on a small granite knoll we could feel safe and watch all the water flow. It was unbelievable to see the flowing torrent of water the width of our little valley that dropped off into the big meadow. Using binoculars I could see water carving deep gullies down the middle of the county road. It was not scary because we were sitting in a warm and safe place but I was concerned about anyone getting in or out of the mountains except by airplane.

When Dick finally made it home he told of washouts, mudslides and road cave-ins. The next day we all went to town together and we were able to drive our VW van three feet down inside of one washout area right up the middle of the road way. That was so awesome! The extreme damage everywhere was a sight I had never seen before. Thankfully no one was injured and no major property damage. If that had been in a highly populated area it would have been on the news broadcasts.

Before we had moved into our big house one night we had a real bad rain storm. Dick had made a loft above the main part of the cabin where we had our bed and we had just gone to bed when we heard a drip, drip sound. Sure enough we had a leak in the roof and it was the middle of the night. Dick suggested that I get a bucket or large kettle that he would place between his legs for the night and we would take care of the leak in the daylight. Our roof was an extreme steep pitch since the cabin was A-frame and would be very slick in the rain and maybe it would be clear tomorrow. I slept just fine but Dick was always aware of that kettle between his legs and couldn't move. When morning came the kettle was so full of water we could not move the kettle without spilling some water. I was laughing so hard at Dick trying to get out of bed that I almost fell down our ladder to the main floor. The boys always loved that story of Dad getting his bed wet!!

One holiday weekend, Washington's Birthday, we had a big snow storm that dropped more than five feet of snow overnight. The two couples that owned the little general store had come up the mountain for the weekend. When we all woke up to the piles of snow everywhere they called us on the CB radio to see if we were alright. We were just fine but they were a bit scared of being snowed in with all their children and no fresh foods for more than two days. So I suggested we bring over our fresh food to the store and we would all have a huge "camp out on the floor of the store" party. I also had many school type Zerox papers for math, language arts and a lot of craft projects for children. So I took along some good children's books, with all my other school stuff and food and we set off for the general store, only two miles from our house.

We had a terrible time trying to drive with the snow depth over the hood of our four wheel drive vehicle. It took us a few hours to get to the store and everyone was very happy to see us. The ladies and I set up some fun games for the six children while the men went to get the heavy equipment from the closed up logging camp. Thankfully the camp had a huge tank of diesel fuel so we could keep the equipment running. The three men set out working on the road and took almost a week to finally get all 27 miles open to the highway. The snow fall continued for several days and the drifts were the hardest part to clear away going over the 7500 foot pass. Starting on that Monday morning we held school in the back room of the general store. We had made up lesson plans for each of the grade levels along with reading assignments. Each student had some math, language arts, social studies and reading to accomplish daily. We would take recess breaks and go out to play in the snow. Then return to class work while the snow clothes dried by the wood fired pot bellied stove. In the evenings we would listen to radio shows, play games and have fun making up stories. That was a great week to remember and by the end of it we felt like one big happy family. Our oldest son was in kindergarten that year and our youngest was too young but was given some of the kindergarten lessons to be a part of our temporary remote school. When this was all over the schools in town were very appreciative that we had accomplished so much with the children while being snowed in. The teachers even accepted the made up school work we gave them.

The Nine Mile Canyon Road we traveled to the desert floor was very steep and dropped off on one side into the canyon a thousand feet or more. This was a dirt/gravel road that was narrow and only one lane in places. So when we would have flash flooding the switch back curves could wash out to almost no road at all. We found that if we kept our speed up we could take the inside corners leaning a bit and still make it around them across the washout. That sometimes felt a bit scary but we always made it without harm. Then winter time and our snow storms created a different problem in the canyon. The drifts would get so bad that you could not find a road at all as the mountain seemed to just slope off into the canyon. When plowing down the mountain canyon these corners were so bad in snow drifts that sometimes Dick was trying to plow the mountain down as you could not tell until you hit a hard wall that you were not pushing snow. We would laugh and back up to try a different angle of attack.

One year before our boys were even in school we were all going to town for the day. I would get all the shopping done and visit with a friend until Dick got off work. Anyway, it was snowing hard but only about a foot of snow on the ground as we left home that morning, until we reached Nine Mile Canyon. Then the drifts started and were sometimes very deep. At first we could drive right up against the rock mountainside as it was blown clear and we were driving a VW Bug that was skinny and fit quite well in that small cleared groove. Then we got stuck in a drift. Dick and I got out of the car to shovel the car free and we could go a few more feet before getting stuck again. We left the car running for heat and the radio going to entertain the boys, although they seem to be having much fun watching us freezing outside. Sometimes we had to jack the car up and dig snow out from under it to get free. This process was repeated over and over for more than an hour and still we were only a quarter of the way to the highway. Finally, I was jacking and Dick was taking a quick break to warm his hands when he called to me to get in too. I climbed into the car with the jack handle in my hand and he asked, "Why did you bring that in with you." I answered that I had to because it is frozen to my hand. It took a few minutes to get my hand warm enough to let the handle go. That was really cold and stung too! After four hours we finally made it down to the Shell gas station on the highway where Dick and I shivered for over an hour standing alongside their wood stove. That was another time we came close to real hypothermia. Our boys faired quite well as they had snacks to eat and games to play as they stayed in the car. The topper on that story is the California Highway Patrol came into the station to tell us that the Nine Mile Canyon Road is officially closed now! We told them we already knew that as we just got off the mountain and they did not believe this at first until they heard our story.

Our driving trips up and down the mountain to work were totally uneventful most of the time. Since we spent an hour and a half each way we used the time to talk, play games with the boys, read books aloud or work on school problems. The time always passed quickly. It was a real pleasure to watch the seasons go by with winter snows, wildflowers in the spring, summer even in the heat, and fall when all the animals seem to be moving the most. We loved the times when the ranchers would be moving their cattle to feeding grounds and we would have to drive slowly among the cattle on the road to get past them. One hardly sees a real cattle drive anymore as trucks are used today. Seeing the old Basque sheepherders with their huge flocks of sheep being walked across the desert was very interesting too.

At one point in the 1970's we had a few families that wanted to live on the mountain and since we did not have a school they were sending their children with us to town daily. By then we had traded our VW Bug for a VW van which had seating for eight people, so we had the room to carry the children. We had children from age 5 to 14 riding with us during our 1 ½ hour commute each way. This was quite a challenge at times to keep everyone happy but Dick and I used mental games, singing and story telling to entertain. For example if someone was having problems with math we used math games to help them out, even the younger ones learned from all of this. I would always have a long chapter book to read aloud which kept the children wanting to listen to more each day.

If Dick happened to be running a few minutes early he would wait at the pickup point for the older boys until the set time to go arrived. We only had a problem once with this bus system and that was with the oldest boy of 14. When Dick arrived at the pickup point for the two older boys' one was not there and his brother refused to go home without him, so Dick left. When Dick arrived at their home drop off point he told the parents that they needed to return to town to get their oldest son as he was not at the pickup point today and younger brother would not leave without him. They were very unhappy, to say the least, and immediately took off for town. We never had to wait on a child again as everyone was always present and accounted for. That made a big impression on all the children about being on time!

By now the residents on the mountain had grown to about ten households and still we were the only ones commuting daily to work in town. We suggested that we would not mind bringing up everyone's mail each day but they would have to make all the arrangements with the post office in town. Then we gave them the postal requirements for mail boxes to be placed out along the county road. After work on our way home we picked up the mail in a large canvas bag from the post office and would sort it according to the route on the mountain. Then we stopped at each box along the way to drop off mail and leave notes to pick up any large packages at our home that evening. This system worked very well for all of us because we never went out of our way except to stop and deliver the mail which we continued to do for more than ten years. This was not a paid rural route because we only delivered mail on Monday through Friday. One needed to deliver six days a week to get paid for the system and we refused to do this. Our weekends remained free for us as a family. Often at Christmas time a couple of our neighbors would give us a box of oranges or grapefruits as a thank you for the mail service.

Chapter 5

SCHOOL YEARS FOR WILDERNESS BOYS

Sending ones children off to school is a very hard time for many parents. Your children are leaving your protection and heading out into society for one third of each day where they will be influenced by others and you have no control over any of these influences. We all try to be sure we have built up a good foundation for them at home to be confident and able to choose a good path along the way of growing up but you never know until later in life. The unknown is what is most scary to us. Our values seem so very important to instill in our children.

Our oldest son began kindergarten and would commute down the mountain with his dad each day. Since Dick had to be at work by 7:30am Robert was dropped off at a baby sitter's house and would go to school from there. Then Robert would return to the sitter's house after school until Dick picked him up after work. The family Robert was staying with had been chosen by me but I soon found it to be a bad choice so we located another family. Now Robert had to endure another change in his life only a couple of months from starting school. This new family turned out to be a great choice for him and he blended in just like one of their children. The only bad part was I was not happy, because I was not the one there for him when he needed someone to listen or to care for him. By the time he arrived home in the evening at 6pm he was not interested in sharing with me any of his day and that hurt. At the time I was still working at the local general store on the mountain and caring for our younger son. I did not see any other way to work out this situation for our family.

It was always so great to have school out for the various holidays, breaks and summer time so we could be together again.

When our youngest son started school he too commuted with Dick for a very short time until I could not stand it any longer and I quit my job at the general store so I could go to town daily and take care of my children before and after school. While having several hours a day in town to do nothing and no home there I started feeling very useless just hanging out in the park so I started to volunteer at the elementary school. This was just perfect for me because I was keeping busy, feeling useful and learning so much along the way. Yet I had time for my children and could be with them when they needed me which was so important to me. Eventually this volunteering turned into a job for me at the school library which was just getting started. By the end of the very first school year I was setting up and running the Inyokern Elementary School Library by myself as the librarian had taken another job out of state. This was one of those times that I was in the right place at the right time and fell into a fantastic job for me but it required a lot of education on my part too. My working hours worked out well even though only part time to begin. It was perfect to have the same days off as our children and the school was very accommodating by letting me have the boys with me at school before and after school hours. Of course, the boys never stayed with me every minute as they had Grandpa and Grandma to visit only a couple of blocks away plus friends to play with in the town park right next door to the school yard. I was so blessed to have it all work out so well and continued in this job until we moved to Alaska several years later. This job allowed me to have great influence over many young lives and help them to seek knowledge and adventure. I really loved working with children at school.

Dick and I became very involved with the school activities over the years, acting as chairman of the Halloween Carnival for a few years, Chairman of the Track Meet for a few years and other family community programs like the Christmas Pageant. We spent countless hours helping to set up, run and participate in every program they had. These activities were always fun and the boys were always involved as well. Since it was a small community all generations of people came to all activities even if they did not have any children involved. Sometimes I would get very upset at the lack of parents wanting to help with their children's education and Dick would remind me that all I could do was my best for as many children as I could. One cannot control the other adults in the world.

Raising funds for the many community needs was a top priority for me as well. There was nothing I enjoyed more than helping others in a time of need. We held many rummage sales; bake sales; car washes and so much more. Each time was like the first as the children grew up and moved on in their lives and their siblings came along into ours. We worked with several generations and then began seeing them with their own children! Wow, how the time flew by!! We did not feel any older but all the children were sure growing up.

As our sons' progressed into junior high school and senior high school they became more involved with extra curricular activities. Neither son was interested in team sports but they both enjoyed the one on one or single sport type activity. The oldest was into wrestling and tennis. We attended as many meets as we could, even traveling out of town many times to cheer him on. I never liked wrestling because it is difficult to watch your own child getting hurt and you can not help him but just sit quietly in the stands observing. This sport along with tennis was really good for Robert as he learned to take good care of himself physically. Robert really enjoyed taking all the shop classes he could and wound up doing some beautiful wood working projects. We still use the coffee table, cutting board, corner shelf unit and many other items he made for us. Our youngest son tried wrestling for one semester and did not like it. His interests were mainly in music and arts. So we had several years of orchestra rehearsals and productions as he played the violin in the school orchestra for six years and the Kern County Honor Orchestra for three years. When Jeffrey started loosing interest in the classical music the orchestra played he chose to take up guitar, banjo, and mandolin. As his playing progressed to pretty good we bought him one of each instrument which he played all four instruments the rest of his time living in our home. Jeff composed many songs and loved to sing country and folk music. As an adult he learned to play a bit of keyboard too.

Just like all parents we had our trials and tribulations while raising our children into fine mannered, well respected adults, but we were very lucky to not have any serious problems with them while they were growing up at home with us. We are very proud of how they both grew up to be quite self sufficient adults that can survive anything. We know they can come out of a natural disaster with the skills they learned growing up. They have given us three wonderful grandchildren who are all grown and now we have three great-grandchildren. The family cycle goes on and on....as it should.

We had so many fun, loving, wonderful times with our sons that it is hard to pick a few to share. I will try to relate some of the more memorable ones. The boys were always trying to compete with their dad and our games became real intense at times but when the boys would win it was totally legitimate and never a give away. Dick felt this taught them to really compete and be proud of their wins while still having fun too. One day while I was busy at home, Dick and the boys went down to the river to play for a few hours. It was the middle of winter and when they came home they were quite wet. I asked them what happened and was shocked to find out about the game they played. There was ice on the river but it was broken into large floes and each of them chose a chunk of ice to balance on while throwing rocks at the others ice to sink them. Sort of like a game of battle ships on ice! Well, eventually they all went into the water and that is when they came home. Boys will be boys at all ages!!!

Back in the 1960's and 1970's our little South Fork of the Kern River would freeze over in the winter and we would have so much fun ice skating on the river. We all looked forward to these ice skating days each year but the day came when that river quit freezing over. This happened right after our family received ice hockey sticks and pucks from our friends, Don and Joni McCarthy, at Christmas time. Sometimes friends would join us at the frozen river and we had a camp fire going with hot chocolate to warm up after skating. It was really a lot of fun for all ages.

Many weekends we would have sledding parties out on the plowed county road where we had some very long hills, 11/2 miles, to ride down. We would park one vehicle at the top of the hill and another at the bottom to stop all traffic if anyone came along until we had all the children off of the roadway because you could not see from one end to the other with the many curves in the roadway. We had CB radios in our vehicles for communications at both ends of our sled run. In all the years we did this we only had one obnoxious man who was out for a Sunday drive with his family and demanded to be let through immediately because this was a public road. When we explained to him that the road would be closed if we had not plowed it and the children were sledding right then, he was furious until we invited his son to join in the fun with us. It did not take long for his fury to turn into laughter as he learned to enjoy sledding with his son for the first time in their lives. That turned out to be a very special day for all of us.

One year everyone in our family had received bicycles for Christmas which was a great surprise to our boys. Much to our dismay it had snowed a foot or more the night before Christmas and the boys were so disappointed to not be able to ride their new bikes. So we loaded all the bicycles into our VW van on Christmas afternoon and drove all the way to town to get out on a deserted dirt road so the boys could learn to ride bicycles. Robert took to the bike really fast but we had a good laugh at Jeffrey and his bail off procedure for stopping. He could never remember to back pedal to use the brake so he would slow down and could stop. Instead he would ride along the dirt berm then jump off the bicycle. After many times of the crash landing Jeffrey finally figured it out. Then we had a wonderful time with family bicycling. Christmas dinner waited until the next day for us.

Another time in the summer Dick took the boys out for an extended bicycle ride in the forest. After several hours they returned home pushing one bicycle that looked a little bent. It seems they had been challenging each other to speed contests on a steep winding road and two of them had collided. The worse part was the ruined bicycle was mine. Then they told me that Dick had already straightened out the worst damage!

We all loved to go bicycling either on trails or back roads. So one summer we took our four bicycles and our back packs and headed north to the Mammoth Lakes area to do a trip and even went around the June Lakes Loop. These were the years when people had it in for anyone with a back pack due to the "hippy era" and we found their rudeness to be quite dangerous. Several times we had cars try to run us off the roads or scare the heck out of us by driving really close. They would laugh at us and give us the middle finger hi-sign. We just told our sons to keep riding as those people were very ignorant.

Robert had asked us many times to let him ride his bicycle to school like the other children in town do and for years we had explained that he could not ride from home as it was almost 50 miles one way down a steep canyon dirt road which was very dangerous. Then on April fool's day which happened to be on a Sunday that year the boys had been out riding when Jeffrey returned home for lunch without his brother. I asked him where Robert was and he said, "I don't know but he was riding on the county road towards the pass." We all sat down for lunch and when Robert still wasn't home in a half hour we started out in the car to look for him. Then we saw his bicycle tracks in the road and followed them all the way to the highway which was 27 miles from home. Dick stopped at the Shell service station on the highway to ask if they had seen our son and they answered no. Robert was smart enough to not let them see him because they would have stopped him until we came along. So I got on the pay phone at the station and called the California Highway Patrol to report that our son was on the road somewhere with his bicycle and probably headed for the school. The patrolmen all knew us so we asked him to pick up Robert and scare him a bit. Then we drove on into town where we found Robert and the patrolman in front of the market. The patrolman treated Robert like a runaway and really impressed upon him the importance of his actions today. Then he put Robert in the patrol car and drove away for a few minutes returning Robert to us. The patrolman assured us that Robert was very happy, not a runaway and proud of his accomplishment too. If it had not been so late in the day we would have made him ride all the way home again even if he had to push his bicycle up the canyon road. Instead we gave him a way to work off the extra trouble he caused and fuel spent to retrieve him. Later on we heard from a man that had been driving down the canyon that day when this young boy passed him on a bicycle doing more than 45 miles an hour. Well, that scared the tar out of me.

We allowed our sons to build dirt humps and plywood jumps for an interesting bicycle track on our lower property where they rode for several years. Both boys always wanted more challenge and tried to make it happen. After they were all grown into men they told us about jumping a bicycle off the South Fork of the Kern River Bridge after a dare to each other. Jeffrey was the first to go riding full speed over a hump flying in the air and landing in a heap on the rocks in the water by the bridge. That really hurt and Robert did not follow through and jump too. Sometimes I am amazed that boys ever grow into adults!

Summer vacation times were spent mostly at home on the mountain. The boys would finish their chores then ask me for a picnic lunch so they could ride their bicycles to the river to fish and swim for a while. It was nice to give them some peanut butter and jelly sandwiches, vegetable strips, an apple and some cookies along with a jug of Kool-aid that would tide them over until late afternoon. They carried these items in a fanny pack, tied their fishing poles to the bike and headed out. Looking like two little Tom Sawyers they would return home usually with a half dozen fish or more. They loved to have me cook them for supper because they caught them for the family. Our dog always followed them whenever they left home so I knew they were being looked out for.

Most children grow up wanting a pet and of course we had our wonderful dog, Midnight, who stayed with us for 14 years. The boys wanted a cat and eventually they each had a cat, which turned into many little kittens over the years. I think we furnished most of the barn cats for the ranches on the mountain at that time along with some food for coyotes! The boys came home with ducks one year after a week long visit with friends and we told them that wouldn't work well here with all the coyotes and foxes running around. But they put the ducks in a pen with some feed and water and the next morning we had nothing but a few feathers left and two crying boys!! Sometimes things just don't work out.

When the boys were in elementary school they decided to raise a pig and sell it for money to buy chainsaws to cut firewood for our neighbors. So they found a friend who had some baby pigs about to be weaned from their mother and begged us to let them get one. We told them it was their responsibility to take care of the feeding, cleaning the pen daily and water for the pig and both boys agreed. Then we went to a feed store and found out the cost of feed which made the boys worry about their venture. That week we stopped at a local produce stand in town where I always shopped and asked them what they did with all their trimmings off the fruits and vegetables. When we found they just threw them away we asked if the boys could have them as long as we furnished them with large trash cans to put the scraps in. That really cut down on the pig feed expense for the summer. Anyway, the boys did a great job of raising their pig and in late fall we decided to butcher the pig and purchase the meat from the boys. The evening we were going to kill the pig the boys were a bit upset as they had made a pet out of the pig but out biggest obstacle was the dog who did not want to lose his friend. As Dick walked out to shoot the pig, the dog grabbed Dick's hand with the gun in it as if to stop him. I had to restrain the dog and console two sad boys who tried to hide their eyes but still watched through open fingers. When the first meal from that pig meat was served the boys asked if it were Suzy Q, their pig, and I answered yes. There was some hesitation for a minute then everyone continued eating as Robert said, "Well she sure tastes good." That was the lesson learned of raising animals for food.

Like most young children our boys wanted to have a horse but we could not afford the feed for such an animal. Then one day our local fish and game warden came along and gave our boys one of his pack animals, a darling burro that could carry up to 150 pounds or so. We found that burros, commonly known as a donkey, are much more sure footed on rough terrain than horses and also do not require the more expensive feed so we agreed to let the boys keep the burro, named Barney. Soon we found ourselves building a small shelter for Barney to use in the winter and fencing off an acre for a corral. The next job was driving several miles to some farmland to purchase a year supply of low grade hay. We found it very interesting hauling hay as one starts loading from a tall pile down into the truck and trailer. Then as you get tired you are loading from down low up to the tall pile on your truck and trailer rig. Seems backwards to me as you pitch the one hundred pound bales of hay up more difficultly as you tire out!! Then you drive home and reverse the same process by now leaving one totally exhausted while the boys are still raring to go!! Something is not right with this scene!! We kept the burros for several years. The boys started out with soft saddles and bridles but soon progressed to riding with bridles only. They had so many wonderful adventures riding around in the local ten mile area from our home as they took the burros out to the river and more.

One time I had some complaints from the local cattlemen that our boys were running the fat off their steers while they played the game of cowboys herding so we had to sit down with our sons and have a good talk about cowboy etiquette. Being a boy growing up around cattle can really have it's challenges and so much fun too.

Since we did not have television we would use our evenings playing music on the player piano we had while singing along and accompanying with our instruments too. Sometimes we played board games, card games, dominoes or worked puzzles. All of us enjoyed doing hand crafts so we had leather tooling equipment, beads, loom and other items to come up with many different hand made gifts for grandparents and friends. This was a lot of fun as we worked together around the dining room table laughing and teasing. We use to make most of the personal Christmas gifts added to only a couple of store bought ones. It seemed to make the holidays more special. In fact Dick and I still have many of the items the boys made us over the years.

The big three summer holidays, Memorial Day, Fourth of July and Labor Day, we would get together with a large group of friends over on Horton's Ranch where we would have a full day or two of skeet shooting (firing shot shells at thrown clay pigeons), followed by a fun outdoor barbeque with music around the campfire at evening. Several people played string instruments and we all could sing a long. Since we lived out in the wilderness we always had loaded guns around the house and our sons were taught at a very young age how to handle guns and shoot properly. They would join us in the skeet shooting with their very own shot guns and became quite the competitors. Since purchasing shells was getting expensive with four of us shooting we decided to learn to make our own shells. Dick purchased all the reloading equipment and it became a family project to reload about 1000 shells for each of these holiday weekends. When it involves the whole family it makes it much more fun and doesn't seem like work at all. Hence the saying we taught our children, "many hands make for light work."

Dick and I were also into archery and had a nice archery range set up in our back yard with hay bales for the backdrop. We had paper targets and many target arrows to practice. Eventually we purchased some bows for our sons and taught them to shoot. Dick and I had gone bow hunting a few times for deer and the boys seemed to be interested in learning to do this too. After a couple of years of practice on the archery range we felt they could do this alone so it was not a surprise at all when one day they asked to take the bows out and practice. Little did I know they had already been planning an adventure of their own, as soon as they were out of sight from our house. The boys had become two little Indians going out for a fight over the burros. In other words, the boys took sides in the little valley behind us and began shooting arrows at one another in a pretend game. Sure enough it was not long before they came home asking me to look at Jeffrey's arm. I was busy in the kitchen with my back to the door when I asked what is wrong with Jeff's arm. Robert said he has an arrow sticking in it! Now that got my attention immediately and sure enough as I turned to look at my sons there stood one with an arrow in his forearm. Well, I took him in the bathroom, pulled the arrow out and cleaned the wound thoroughly while getting an explanation of just how this happened. Both boys had the same story and stayed with that story so I was snow balled into believing them. Here is the story: Jeff pulled back to hard on the arrow and it passed the bow letting loose the arrow into his own arm. When Robert demonstrated it seemed plausible and I was a sucker. Dick was furious when he heard the story later that night and said it was plain poppy cock but both boys stuck to it. It wasn't until years later that I learned that they had been actually shooting at each other! Sometimes I wonder how they ever made it to adulthood! From that day on they were never allowed to use the bows and arrows without a parent with them.

Chapter 6

LEARNING TO FLY

Dick and I were getting mighty tired of all the road plowing and neighbors complaining about the road conditions if they were not just perfect and the added cost to our living expenses for fuel. So we commented one day at a neighborhood gathering that we were thinking of learning to fly and then we would only have to plow a runway and save much time and money. Maybe all the neighbors should get together and invest in a snow plow so they could get to town. Everyone laughed because they all thought it was totally impossible to fly in and out of the high sierra mountains daily in the various weather conditions. We asked if anyone had ever tried it and received a loud NO. Well, maybe we should be the ones.

The next weekend we were off to our desert hot springs for a camping trip which was a four hour drive from our home. As we sat in the hot tub an airplane flew in to the hot springs landing strip. We wondered just where the man came from and how long it took him to get here so as soon as he came into camp we asked all these questions and more. Elmer was from up north of San Francisco and took two and a half hours to fly down several hundred miles. We were so impressed and said we would like to learn to fly too. Elmer then offered us a ride in his plane which we were happy to do. After taking off we flew all over the area and landed at a couple of mining camps to meet the miners. This was such fun and seemed so easy. Elmer was convinced that Dick could do this but women were not supposed to be pilots. Well, I informed Elmer that Dick and I will both get our pilot certificate and would soon be flying to the hot springs ourselves. Sounded so good in the telling but then I realized that was quite a big chore to achieve.

When we went home Dick and I talked a lot about this new idea and he said he would check into it at the Navy Base where he worked as they had a flying club. That week Dick informed me that he could join the Navy flying club and even take their ground school because he was an employee on the base but I could not. I was so disappointed at the time. Dick did find out that I could attend the ground school with him so we enrolled in that school together which was a four hour, one night a week for thirteen weeks class. I had made arrangements for one of the teachers at the elementary school where I worked to watch our two boys that evening for the next thirteen weeks. We all ate dinner together before Dick and I headed off going to school and the boys loved watching television that one night a week so everyone was happy.

In the meantime, I had walked out to the airport in Inyokern to see if they had a flying school where I could take instruction and how much would it cost. Well I was happy to learn it was available but quite scared at the cost to learn. That evening I talked to Dick about it and he said go ahead and start. We will just plan our budget to get in one lesson a week each and eat more hamburger or macaroni. If something comes up and we can't fly one week it is not the end of it at all but we will persevere and eventually get our license to fly. Dick started his lessons immediately but I still procrastinated until one day after work we drove to the Inyokern airport instead of directly home. Dick asked them to give me an introductory flight which I went on right then. Oh, I was scared but also very determined and when the instructor tried to scare me to death because I was a woman that just got my hackles up all the more. After landing I went into the office and asked to be put on a schedule for lessons to start next week.

My first official flight school lesson came and I had been assigned the same instructor as I had for my introductory flight. Somehow I had the feeling he had bets going with the mechanics in the hangar on my suitability for flight because he did everything in his power to get me to quit. After my hour long flight I headed for the restroom where I could hear all the laughter in the hangar and sure enough the men thought I was done now. So I proceeded into the office and asked for a better more professional instructor since the man I flew with felt women shouldn't be in the pilot seat.

I was given a new instructor who lasted through my entire flight lessons over a period of seven months. He was gracious, patient and very good at keeping ones perspective in order so that the learning could continue in a meaningful way.

To say the least, our next seven months were very busy with the extra school one night a week, homework during the week and flying in the afternoons but we both worked together and helped each other make it through until the glorious day we both received our certified pilot licenses on April 2, 1973. I think it was a first husband and wife team locally to be licensed on the same day. We were riding high that day and took the boys out to dinner to celebrate with surf and turf dinner at the Indian Wells Lodge. We couldn't wait to take our sons for their first airplane ride the coming weekend when we drove to town and Dick met me at Inyokern airport with his flying clubs AA1A trainer. I was flying a Cessna 150. We each took one son and flew off into the sky to play and have some fun. Then we returned to the airport and exchanged sons so they had a chance to ride with each of us for a half hour. That was all we could afford right then. Our sons were ten and eight years old at the time and that began a whole new way of life for us.

By the time school started that September we found an advertisement for a Cessna 170A down in San Diego that was for sale. Dick and I pooled all our resources and came up with a total of thirteen dollars altogether but decided we could use our VISA card for fuel and we set off for San Diego to see the airplane. We looked at the plane, took a short flight in it and fell in love with it. Then we asked the lowest price acceptable before we said YES WE WILL BUY IT. We told the man we needed time to go to the credit union and make financial arrangements but would be back in a couple of weeks to pay for it. Then we drove away bursting with happiness.

As we drove off I asked Dick, "Well how are we going to do this and what do we do now?" He replied, "Don't worry right now. We are in San Diego and I think we should take the boys to the zoo, observatory and Balboa Park." So that is what we did and the boys had a great time. We camped out and ate sandwiches before returning home after a fun weekend.

On Monday during Dick's lunch hour he went to the credit union to find out if we could get a loan for an airplane and they said yes for eighty percent of the cost so he applied for the loan. Almost two weeks later he was called to come in and pick up his check for the airplane and as soon as the check was in his hand he asked to apply for a signature loan for one thousand dollars. The loan officer asked what he wanted it for and Dick said the remaining price on the airplane and registration. The loan officer told Dick he could not do that as they would be paying fully for the airplane. Then Dick stated that your rules do not say that at all. If I wanted to get a signature loan for a vacation you would grant it correct, so I want that amount. Anyway, it was taken up with the board and sure enough they could not discriminate on why for a signature loan if a person was eligible, so we received the second check in time for Dick to go to San Diego to pick up our airplane. We made plans for insurance on the airplane and the company told Dick he needed to get ten hours of instruction in the plane before taking command because it was a tail dragger and we did not have any experience in that type of craft. So through telephone calls we arranged for ten hours of instruction for Dick in San Diego that weekend and then he flew home to the High Sierra Mountains at Horton's Ranch in OUR AIRPLANE. Everyone was so excited and all our neighbors had gathered over at Horton's Ranch to watch Dick fly in for the first time. I was only hoping that he wouldn't have an accident and all would go well, which it did. You can imagine the roar of the crowd when Dick touched down like a real professional pilot. Everyone celebrated with us that night. September 27, 1973 we had our very first airplane which would stay in our family for the next 26 years giving us so much adventure and making commuting to work so much easier. Dreams really do come true when one works hard enough.

The very next morning, a Sunday, we packed a picnic lunch and climbed into the airplane with our sons to fly off to our desert hot springs taking less than 45 minutes to get there where we landed to have a good soak for a bit before returning home. Dick took a friend up at the hot springs for several practice landings and take offs from the very rough, short airstrip. Then we loaded up and headed home after a fantastic afternoon at the hot springs. We were so excited to have accomplished such a feat in a very short time—less than a year altogether from wishing to making it happen.

This was the beginning of our sons flying to school daily with their parents as we did commute by airplane from September 27, 1973 until Dick retired in 1994. Dick and I took turns flying to town and back so we could both get in some good log book time. It was an extremely interesting learning curve as we took on the high winds and storms of the sierra wave conditions, because no one had ever done this before on a daily basis and could give us any pointers on the "how to part of flying" in the sierra wave. We asked many pilots from the local area around town about flying into the sierras and they all replied the same way. DO NOT FLY WHEN THE SIERRA WAVE IS GOING. Well that was unacceptable to us because we live up there and wanted to go home every night. So we persisted and learned on our own, sometimes scaring the heck out of ourselves. We could write a book about the many things we learned flying in that area but that is another time.

As we gained in experience and our luck bag was still holding out we both became very proficient at flying in and around the local deserts and high mountains in winds, snow and pouring rains. Since we flew at least five days a week we had a good knowledge of the many ridges and valleys so as the daylight shortened we became accustomed to the looks of things in dimmer lighting and managed to keep flying even when it got dark out. The star light would reflect off the river and we could line ourselves up with the runway using the lights from Horton's window too. Then we decided we needed to invent a remote runway lighting system where there is not any power available. Dick came up with a 12 volt car battery (in a waterproof metal milk crate with a top) to power the system which consisted of a Radio Shack receiver with the antenna extended in a sealed PVC pipe, to keep it dry, running a circuit board Dick designed to turn on a string of white Christmas tree lights that bordered both sides of the first 400 feet of runway. The receiver was tuned to 122.8 aircraft frequency so we could call on our aircraft radio to activate the light circuits and the system would turn everything on, remaining on for five minutes before shutting off. This allowed us time to come in at an altitude above all the mountain ridges turn the lights on and circle down over the end of the runway to come in and land. Dick made about three or four of these lighting systems for various people over the years. Everything worked out perfectly and we were able to come in on cloudy nights and even stormy nights without any trouble. We did have one neighbor that swore Dick had an in with "the man upstairs" because he seemed to watch the clouds part or snow stop for a few minutes before we landed every time there was a storm going on and it would proceed to close in as soon as we were down. This made us laugh but I think that man believed it. In fact he use to bet his visitors on a dark stormy night that at 5 pm they would see a small plane fly in and land when he knew we would be there. The visitors always lost the bet too!

By the mid-1970's we soon had another couple that had moved up the mountain and loved to fly their Stinson 108 plane. Both John and Janice were pilots too and we would enjoy many outings with our planes together. One year we had a really deep snow fall over one day while we were at work and with the storm still raging we decided to drive up the mountain to plow our runway clear. As luck would have it we could not get home due to the heavy drifting of snow so Dick had a plan. Tomorrow, which was a Friday, we would fly into the mountains and he would jump from our plane onto the runway where he could plow it clear for me to fly in with our boys later in the day. As we checked out this idea more and tried to acquire a parachute everyone turned us down saying we were going to be hurt. That did not stop Dick from finding another plan of action. We would drive as far as we could get up into the mountains where Dick and our flying neighbor, John, would start walking on snow shoes to John's cabin as it came before our home. The two would then drive over to our runway where our snow plow sat and proceed to clean the runway off so that I could fly home with our sons and Janice, John's wife by noon the next day. We were able to get almost to the top of the pass about nine miles from John's cabin before we were stuck. The men got our vehicle turned around and headed down the hill before they set off on their snow shoes for a long hike in the moonlight. It must have been close to 9pm at this time. Well, it took them a full nine hours to walk that distance due to the deep snow drifts and breaking a trail which is quite exhausting. Then the two men fell asleep for a while at John's warm cabin. Janice and I returned to town with my sons and stayed the night at my mother's house.

Early in the morning we were all up and ready to go flying but my poor mother was having a terrible time accepting the fact that we were going off into the mountains that were covered with snow and did not even have a MAN WITH US!! Well, that didn't bother us at all because we were only flying home but then we could not call anyone if we had a problem, or even if we did not, as there was no telephone service on the mountain at that time. I managed to be flying over the ranch runway right at noon just as Dick was making his last pass with the snowplow. What a beautiful runway we had and a great landing with a special welcome from two very happy men!! We love it when a plan comes together!

We always proclaimed that owning an airplane was like having a magic carpet as any ordinary weekend became special when one could fly hundreds of miles for an occasion and return home by Sunday evening rested and ready for work on Monday. We absolutely loved flying and all it gave to our family over the years. Even our sons loved flying and our oldest son took his solo flight on his 16th birthday. Now if you think having your son drive your car alone at 16 is nerve racking, try watching him take off in an airplane alone and you are hoping he has learned well enough to bring it all back to earth in one piece. It was one of those bitter sweet times in life when you are very proud of your son but scared to death at the same time. That was another night of celebration at the local restaurant for dinner.

We had a chance to float the Grand Canyon in Arizona with

friends for four days when they drove there and set up a camp with all the rafts and gear. We flew in one evening and joined them after leaving our airplane tied down on top of a plateau. They had small out board engines on the three twelve foot rafts and we motored up the river about 100 miles before floating down in silence. Going up was a real challenge like a salmon swimming up the rapids and such. Quite an adventure as the river climbs many feet in places. We flew back home at the end of our river trip and they took two days getting back. Oh how we loved our little plane.

One thing we learned almost immediately was that when one is flying in the bush country with little or no runways you will have a few minor mishaps now and then. Our first big problem was right on our home runway during the first big snow storm. We had not plowed the runway wide enough and managed to catch a main landing gear in the snow berm which pulled us over to the side and since the runway was on a steep downhill we slowly laid over onto the right wing with our tail high in the air. It all happened so slowly and easy that no one was hurt, except for Dick's pride, and we all parted from the plane immediately because fuel was running down the windshield. We did not want to have a fire start with us in the plane. Actually Dick told the boys to get out now and they both said they could not get their seat belts open. Dick yelled for them to push against the back of the front seats to relieve the pressure on the belts and both boys said. "We aren't supposed to put our feet on the seats." Dick was frustrated now and told them this is no time to argue with me just do what I said and get out. At this time they knew Dick was serious and they moved very quickly. We laughed about it later. Then we spent a few hours with some neighbors, the Hortons and Heflins, trying to help us lasso the tail wheel on the airplane that now stood on it's nose with the tail about 20 feet in the air. We finally managed to get a rope around the tail wheel to pull the airplane back down to the ground so we could tow it up the runway to the parking space. Seeing the right wing all turned up in the middle was very upsetting. We are very thankful that only some aircraft parts were damaged but all of the family was just fine.

The very next weekend, after we had called our insurance company, Dick and I proceeded to remove the bent up wing and propeller. We took the wing on a trailer down to Bishop, California, where it was to be rebuilt. Instead we wound up getting a replacement wing off of another aircraft like ours so we could be back in the air very soon. The propeller was sent to Santa Monica, California for repairs or replacement. It was not long before we were all fixed and back in flying mode and the insurance company paid for all of it. The only bad part was that the FAA (Federal Aviation Administration) kept bugging us via phone calls at work for several months after the incident. Sometimes I wished we had never reported to them in the first place but we wanted to keep it all legal. The FAA just could not understand why they did not show us having checked on the weather before flight nor did we have a filed flight plan. What could they not understand about living and flying off of a remote area that had no telephone services? Besides the day was sunny and clear with no winds so weather did not even factor into the problem. It was very frustrating for us to deal with the FAA..

Our airplane became our vehicle of choice for all travel after that first year. We would fly down to Van Nuys, California about 1 ½ hours away just to go shopping for the many items not available in our small desert community only 50 miles from home. Sometimes we would surprise old friends or family members by showing up at the nearest general aviation airport to them so we could visit and take them out to dinner. But the general use of the airplane was daily commuting to work and school. It was our car so to speak and so much more economical to use when living far out off the grid.

In the winter of 1976/77 we started planning "our trip of a lifetime" to Alaska. Dick had started to make this trip with a friend after his Navy career when we met and married which put the trip on a back burner for a while. Now the time has come to make the great adventure only using our Cessna 170 with our backpacks and tents. We sat many evenings with the boys planning our routes and things or places we wanted to see along the way. The decision was made to take the whole summer of 1977 as the boys and I were free then. Dick would use up all his leave time plus a bit of leave without pay so we would have about two and a half months for travel. As soon as school was out in June we were all packed and ready to go. One of my co-workers, a teacher, Mike Neely, was staying at our house to take care of it and the animals while we were away. Several of our neighbors came over to the runway to bid us a farewell and see if we really could get off the ground with the load we had. The excitement was running very high that morning as we flew off into the wild blue yonder! Oh the joys of flying into the unknown are something very hard to describe but all four of us were bubbling over right now.

We did spend the whole summer as we flew up the inside passage stopping at the many towns along the way to explore, viewing the glaciers up close and so much more. Places like Ketchikan, Juneau, Sitka, Wrangell, Petersburg, Skagway, Haines, Yakutat, Cordova, Valdez, Homer, Kenai and more. Then travel into the huge metropolis of Anchorage and the Mat-Su Valley before reaching Denali National Park. Fairbanks became our base point for most of the summer where we could pick up supplies and mail drops from home. In the interior we flew to Nenana, Lake Minchumina, Galena, Nome, Kotzebue, Ambler, and many hot springs along the way. Other times we flew to Fort Yukon, Bettles, Barrow and the north slope of the Brooks Range. Everywhere we went we met wonderful local people, learned so much about the various cultures and ate foods unknown to us. We covered so much of Alaska except in the extreme western part around Bethel and such.

Living out of tents under the wing of our airplane for more than two months and over 10,000 miles was a bit of a challenge but we established a good routine and stuck to it. The boys pitched their tent on one side of the airplane and ours was on the other side. We cooked our meals over a campfire or on a Coleman stove, eating out only rarely. Laundry and showers were done in towns or just on the rivers where we camped. We tried to take in as many of the tourist attractions as we could but the most memorable times were just ones that happened in the many small villages or out of the way places we managed to find.

Our family really fell in love with Alaska the last frontier by the time we were to start our return trip home. The southern flight took us along the Alaskan Highway route to many wonderful places through Canada's Yukon and British Columbia. We have many wonderful stories of our travels that year and the memories we built with our two boys during the summer of 1977.

Learning to fly was not easy and took a lot of perseverance but was more than worth it in the end results. Flying has brought us so many wonderful adventures all across America and Canada. That old 1950 Cessna 170A had more than 300,000 miles on it by us alone at the time we sold it. One of the best investments we ever made in our life!

Chapter 7

1977 ALASKA TRIP JOURNAL

6-17-77 Friday. Well school is out for the summer now and we are making a dream trip to Alaska. After dinner tonight we took all our gear over to our Cessna 170A airplane to get it all loaded and ready for an early morning departure tomorrow. Many of our neighbors, Hortons, Zenors, Hobbs and Mike Neely, were out there with us to watch and are sure that we would never get all that stuff in the plane. It was really quite fun and many laughs for everyone!

6-18-77 Saturday. Mike Neely, one of the teachers I worked with at Inyokern School, is going to spend the summer in our house and take care of the dog and cats. Mike drove us over to the plane about 6:30am where we found Zenors and Hobbs waiting for us too. The Hortons were out on their front porch. I'm not sure if all this was not to watch a crash as they are all concerned about our getting airborne with such a load. We figured many times the weight and balance of the plane and know we are good to go. We were so excited as we departed Kennedy Meadows at 6:55am. Alaska here we come! We stopped for fuel in Hawthorne, Nevada and met a man there in a Cessna 170 from Alaska. Now that was really a great start for our journey. After a short rest we headed for Alturas, CA. We walked into town for exercise and some lunch. After arriving back at the airport we really felt so good and it was so early that we all decided to head for Hood River, Oregon. It is a shame to waste good weather down here. We arrived in Hood River about 4:30pm, fueled the plane and walked to a local market to purchase our dinner and breakfast supplies. Today we flew over some beautiful country and with very good weather. We did have some moderate turbulence on our last leg which was very tiring.

6-19-77 Sunday. After a good breakfast in the shade of the airplane wings we took a lovely walk around the south end of Hood River. We had to waste time because of the fogged in conditions in Washington. This is beautiful farming country around here. The boys couldn't get over the size of the Columbia River which forms the border between Oregon and Washington. Our river at home was almost dry when we left there! We finally started to get good weather reports from Washington so we departed Oregon about 11am. We had to drop down under the fog layer at Seattle and the visibility was very poor. We sure found it difficult to navigate over the big city! We stopped for fuel at Anacortes, WA, which sits on a little island in Puget Sound. While here, our last stop in the USA, we checked with the US Customs at the ferry dock to register our gun and cameras. Then we changed our plans of travel and headed for Victoria on Vancouver Island, British Columbia in Canada, because it is Sunday and they have the only Canadian Customs Officials on duty 18 hours a day, seven days a week. The boys enjoyed the experience of the Canadian Customs check in. The officials were all very friendly and courteous. It was still early in the day and we do not like being in big cities so we flew up the island to Campbell River, a community about half-way up the island of Vancouver. Oh, the country is so beautiful around here with islands galore that are loaded with huge trees right down to the waters edge. Heaven help us if we have an engine problem as one would have to either land in the tree tops or in the water! It is fun to watch the many ferries and tug boats that are pulling barges. We really like the thousands of log barges that are moved via the water. We rented a car in Campbell River and drove around some. Tonight we camped in a place that had showers and laundry facilities which we took advantage of. It is pouring rain tonight but then that is what keeps this area so green and lovely. One thing that we did not like so far is the strip or clear cut logging operations as it leaves the countryside looking so scared and ugly.

6-20-77 Monday. We left Campbell River this morning in limited ceilings for Port Hardy, which sits at the north end of Vancouver

Island. After eating lunch at the airport café we decided to head on to Bella Coola, BC, on the Canadian mainland. Speaking of airports in Canada we find the have the nicest planned and cleanest airports we have ever seen. The only problem with them is that they sit so darn far out of town.

6-20-77 cont. Our flight to Bella Coola was still in limited ceilings with pouring rain adding to our challenge of navigation up the inside passage to Alaska. We were following the waterways at or below 2000 feet. Bella Coola sits in a valley very much like Yosemite and is quite beautiful! This was a quick fuel only stop. Then due to the weather we made another change of plans and headed for Prince Rupert, BC, our last stop before Alaskan soil. On this flight to Prince Rupert our 2000 feet altitude soon became 500 feet off the water where we stayed for more than three hours just following the waterways. Later we learned that we had actually followed the exact inside passage route that the cruise ships and ferries take to and from Seattle and Alaska. We were very impressed by the number of small communities throughout this area. Everything seems to be growing in each town too. Our navigation skills are really being tested and we haven't been lost yet! In Prince Rupert the town and the airport are on separate islands and when we arrived the airport was deserted. We finally met a flight instructor with a student who offered us a ride in his beautiful yacht over to the town. That was a fun trip. Then we enjoyed walking around the town some before finding a room at the Drifter Hotel. We had a most delicious seafood dinner and then settled down in our room for some TV this evening. It is still pouring rain.

6-21-77 Tuesday. We woke up to the sound of pouring rain STILL and very rotten visibility. We sat around watching TV and writing postcards most of the morning. Then we took a walking tour of town, mailed off our card and checked out the banks for a silver dollar for Les Hill. We wandered through the museum and a small shopping mall. This is quite a town with about 20,000 people and very modern. We purchased some groceries at a Safeway and headed for our hotel room. About 5pm the weather began to look better so we took the airport bus and ferry back to the airport on Digby Island. This is the last ferry to run until 10am tomorrow as they only run when an airline comes in (not very often). After getting a weather briefing, flight plan filed and plane fueled we found that is was to late for the US Customs in Ketchikan, Alaska. So we are laying over right here in the airport lounge area sleeping on the couches until daybreak. It really is very quiet and comfortable. We met the Canadian FAA man who is on duty and he is sure a character to talk to. He even offered us some hot tea for refreshment!

6-22-77 Wednesday. We arrived in Ketchikan and experienced US Customs again. They could sure take some lessons from the Canadians on being nice to the public. We are getting to feel very comfortable flying in adverse weather over all the water as that is all they seem to have up here! We took the ferry from the airport to town where we had a nice walking tour, visited the museum and many other points of interest. We find that we get so involved looking and doing things that we forget to take pictures! One of the locals directed us to a quaint little pizza place on some sort of side street alley. The pizza was delicious and the local conversations were great too. Next we flew on to Wrangell where we met a couple that drove up to the airport and started talking with us as we pitched our tent under the plane wings. Dave Werner and his wife have lived here for many years and they told us all about the logging industry before giving us a ride into town. Dave flies for the logging executives and has a sideline business as an aircraft mechanic. We then took a walking tour of the town and bought some groceries, which, by the way, are not much higher in price than Ridgecrest. At this time we returned to the airport and our camp where we had dinner during a short break in the rain. We had just retired to the tent for our nightly cribbage tournament against the boys when a couple drove up in a pick up truck and asked if we would like a driving tour of the island, all 11 miles of road, 6 which are even paved! We had a grand time them and got a vivid account of all the sights around. We also went to the museum where we were introduced to a lady who had lived on the island for more than 60 years. She really had some interesting stories to tell and we listened to her for hours. Our new friends, Joe and Kathy, then returned us to the airport where we had a snack and our cribbage game. It now gets dark about 11:30pm which is nice for late night games in the tent.

6-23-77 Thursday. We left Wrangell early this morning for the town of Petersburg which is just a short hop away. Petersburg is known as Alaska's little Norway with a very high concentrate of Norwegians and their culture. The buildings and décor are all Norwegian motif with lots of flowers which if very lovely. The signs are in both Norwegian and English. We took a walking tour once again and found the downtown area to be very quaint, old fashioned and beautiful with all the bright colors. The main source of income here is from commercial fishing. Canneries adorn the piers and boats are in and out continually. We bought some groceries and ate our lunch in a little gazebo right on the main street. It was fun to just watch the local people go about their business. This afternoon we took off and headed for Sitka which we had been told in California that we could not fly in to because of the adverse weather. Sitka is a Russian Orthodox dominate town and was once the capital of this territory. The architecture is fabulous, especially the church in the center of town with all the gold onion domes and the old fort. We spent most of the day wandering around walking and listening to the people. We felt good and the weather was obliging so we flew on to Juneau for the night and our second hotel room. We got a "GIP" ride into town which is only nine miles at $3.00 per person. It was getting late so we immediately got a hotel room and went out to dinner. Thanks to the young man at the hotel desk we had pizza in a super little place on an alley that all the locals go to. They even had silent movies playing on the walls and huge pitchers of cola or beer to share with your pizza. This was a lot of fun for all four of us. Back in our hotel room we all had showers before enjoying a good movie on TV. Then we passed out as it was quite late.

6-24-77 Friday. We spent the whole day touring Juneau, Alaska's capital city. They have the greatest walking tour with some of the street being actually wood stairways because the town is built on the mountain side. There is a fantastic museum, the best we have seen so far and we were in it for a long time. The general consensus of the residents here is that the idea of moving the state capital to Anchorage which seems to be on the ballots lately is absolutely preposterous! We thought it may be a good idea because Anchorage is where more than half of the states population reside but what do we know about their politics? We found a laundry and washed all our dirty clothes before having some lunch on the dock. We all enjoyed sitting and watching the boat and float plane traffic along with the sea birds. We learned from a young man in the laundry about the city bus system and so we took a bus from the town center out to the Mendenhall Glacier and back to the airport for a total cost of only $2.40 for all four of us. Now we know for sure that we had been taken by the taxi cab driver when we arrived here. Boy, were we ever ticked off at him too! The weather has been very nice today. We departed for Skagway about 8pm and sure enough it started to rain! We did have sunshine when we got to Skagway. We then set up our camp under our wings on a lovely grassy lawn type area. This town has already been voted THE BEST YET by our family—a perfect atmosphere! It is like stepping back to the turn of the century with all the old style buildings and a steam train. We will probably stay here a few days.

6-26-77 Sunday. We have spent the last two days in Skagway just having fun. We took the White Pass &Yukon railroad up to Lake Bennett and had a delicious "gold rush" lunch of stew, beans, sourdough bread, apple pie and coffee. This was a great six hour trip in an old narrow gauge passenger train with the pot bellied stove going in the corner and all! Wow, what a fun experience! This is the only working narrow gauge railroad lift in operation. It follows the old 1898 gold rush trail over the White Pass from

Skagway to Whitehorse, Yukon. The scenery is spectacular, some of which we hope we caught on film. It was pretty cloudy and misty as we climbed up the narrow valley towards Lake Bennett, the halfway point of the trip. When we got back into town we had a fun time touring the little town and talking with some of the local residents, one a very charming Tlingit Indian. We sure love this town and the atmosphere. It is so like living in the early 1900's.

6-26-77 cont. This morning we all seemed to sleep in until 9:30am and then enjoyed a leisurely breakfast followed by taking spit baths and changing our clothes. We then took all our dirty things down to the laundry which was only $2.25 to wash and dry two loads, now that is very cheap. We sat around talking with the many local people in the laundry and it all ended to soon for us. The next few hours we spent in the museum which was full of history and photos of those times. On our way back to camp we found an ice cream parlor so we stopped for a treat which tasted extra good. When we arrived back at our camp we had our dinner, cleaned the camp up and got organized for the night. Then we took a nice walk and went to the "Days of '98 Show" in one of the saloons. This was really fun and takes place in an old 1898 saloon/boarding house from the gold rush days. We were each given $1000.00 in play money upon entering and you had 45 minutes to gamble like the old timers in black jack, roulette, craps and poker, while listening to a group play all turn of the century songs. It was great and we could even sing along with most of the music! Everyone turned his winnings in to the judge and the person with the most won a prize. Now the show started with two short plays, some good old fashioned music, can-can dancing and more. It turned out to be a great entertaining and fun evening for all ages. Jeff was put in a play type jail for punching his mother in the arm and he was fined 15 cents. Richard was a poker player during one of the stage plays, THE SHOOTING OF DAN MCGREW. This all lasted until 10pm. Then we went back to our camp and had some hot tea and cookies before bedtime.

6-27-77 Monday. Today we wandered around town and visited with more local people. You can really get to know a place from spending time talking with the local residents. Then we took a lovely hike up to lower Dewey Lake. Dick and the boys tried fishing but had no luck! We hiked on to Icy Lake and then Reid Falls. This is beautiful rain forest country located in the Tongas National Forest. The ferns, flowers and other ground growth is extraordinary. We saw some turn of the century all wood water pipes. It was surprising to see how they were made and the distances the pipes ran to bring water to the town. All in all it was a great hike and only about 6 miles altogether. The feeling you get when walking through the thick woods is so beautiful. Upon our return to town we went to the "Sweet Tooth Saloon" for hamburgers and ice cream. Each of us was glad to get to bed about 10pm.

6-28-77 Tuesday. We all washed up and had a leisurely breakfast before packing our camp up. Dick fueled the plane and we were ready to pull out about 11:30am. We received our first special VFR clearance to leave Skagway. We flew to Yakutat for fuel and lunch. This is a very small fishing village on the Pacific Coast. Then we flew over Yakataga on the way to Cordova. What an interesting landing this was with the runway and highway part of the same paved area. You land and proceed to taxi across the roadway to park and tie down. There are signs telling the car traffic that airplanes have the right of way and proceed with caution. On the other side of the runway is water. We took a nice walking tour of Cordova and visited their museum. This too is a small fishing community with very friendly people. After a short stop here we flew on to Valdez for fuel but did not go into the town. The old town was abandoned after the 1964 earthquake demolished most of it. The new town that was built up is very modern but didn't seem to interest us. We could not believe the number of huge storage tanks and piers for ships to support the oil coming down from the north. This is the end of their 800+ miles of pipeline where all the oil loads onto tankers to be shipped away. We flew on to Anchorage, which is just a huge city like Los Angeles full of people, except the surrounding countryside is so beautiful and remote. There are millions of small airplanes and airports all around Alaska. We can sure understand that this is the best mode of transportation in a land of very few roads. We walked across the highway from the airport and got a motel room for the night. It felt great to all get showers, clean clothes and a meal out at the restaurant before falling into bed around midnight. Our flying today took us over some of the most spectacular, rugged mountains that are very high and covered with glaciers.

6-28-77 Cont. The shapes and forms of these glaciers with their deep crevasses and boulders is awesome! The icebergs were really fantastic as well. We even saw some seals floating on icebergs. You just can't believe the colors in the glacier ice from shades of blue to deep yellows and pink. Glacier Bay itself was not any more extraordinary than other bays with glaciers running into them but seems to be more accessible so is widely known.

6-30-77 Thursday. Yesterday we rented a car in Anchorage and drove all around visiting sites of interest. We roamed through Earthquake Park which is an area that sank into the ocean after the quake in 1964 destroying many homes. The ground just turned to mush and washed away. After a stop at the local big Sears and Montgomery Wards stores we discussed how disappointing it was to find almost the same types of merchandise for sale as in the lower 48 states. I found a parka in an Eskimo shop that we all liked very much but quite expensive. These parkas are made individually and tailored to your body. That is what we will get when we move up here someday. I have the ladies name and address for the future. We camped at Goose Lake last night and it was really neat to sit among millions of mosquitoes and not get bit! I just love that good repellant cream we have. None of the four of us were really impressed with Anchorage except to say it is surrounded by some beautiful country. It is too much like being in any huge city in the lower 48. We flew out this morning for an interesting flight down the Kenai Peninsula to Homer. Homer is a lovely village with an unusual five mile long spit of sand that runs out into the bay.

6-30-77 cont. We walked out to the end of the spit and viewed the hundreds of bald eagles that hang out there. An old lady has been feeding them fish scraps from the local cannery for many years now. The hillsides of the mainland are covered with small cabins with even one section of fantastic homes like Beverly Hills. I finally flew again today since the weather was really beautiful—I seem to be a fair weather pilot! We then flew up the other side of the Kenai Peninsula to Seward and on to the Mantanuska Valley where we landed at Palmer. Palmer had just repaved their taxi way and it was so black and lovely that I landed on that instead of the actual runway as it looked best to me. We had a great laugh about that for a while! We walked around Palmer before having dinner at 9:30pm in a café close to the airport. We set up our camp in a nice campground on the edge of town at the airport. We were very surprised to find that only about one third of the valley is actually farmed today and the town of Palmer is a tiny community about the size of Inyokern. There is a lot of forest and wilderness in this valley still.

7-1-77 Friday. We have met some of the neatest people in every town as we are camping and visiting so many places other than tourist traps. You really get into many interesting talks with the local people and learn so much about each unique area. We went to the Palmer visitors center and museum this morning. They had a lovely slide show which we all enjoyed and then we had a good discussion time with some of the local young people. The flight from Palmer to Talkeetna to visit the famous bush pilot Don Sheldon's stomping grounds was quite fast and easy. Talkeetna is a neat little community with only a few shops and businesses. It is the take off point for the many expedition climbs up Mt. McKinley. The four of us spent quite some time looking at things in the General Store and I even bought a cast iron stove top waffle grill that I have wanted for years. It was mailed to our home address. We had dinner in the famous "Roadhouse" where this elder couple has been fixing meals on a large wood cookstove and serving them family style at a long table for more than 30 years now. It was all quite delicious and all homemade even down to the bread and jam. After dinner we flew on to Denali National Park to get our camp set up in time for our nightly game of cribbage along with a couple of Oreo cookies each. This has become a ritual with us and the boys challenge us at cribbage! With all the extra sunshine and daylight up here it is so easy to stay up late but boy do we ever conk out when we finally go to bed.

7-4-77 Monday. We have been at McKinley Park the last three days in a walk-in tents only campground. We met some neat people here and we all took a ten hour bus tour of the park two days ago which was really great. We saw a lot of grizzly bears, caribou, moose, Dall sheep, beavers and many birds. Of course the biggest thing was actually seeing THE MOUNTAIN. The weather was beautiful for us and we understand that it was the first day in about a week that it has been clear. Only about one quarter of the people who visit the park, ever see the actual mountain in full view due to the extreme weather created by the mountain. Yesterday we attended a history talk at the Riley Creek campground followed by a great slide show at the McKinley Hotel. The slide show was the beautiful winter at McKinley. It made you want to be here for the winter fun! We went to the Rangers headquarters to learn about dog sledding in the park and they gave a fantastic lecture on dogs, equipment and how they all work together. We even saw how to make dog sleds and harnesses. Boy, are we ever ready to try it!!

7-4-77 Today. I had to get our checks written to pay the Visa and Chevron bills before we headed out. Need to keep affairs in order and paid on time. There is mail service here at the visitors center. Our personal checks are not accepted here so we must get cash through our Visa card. We have spent almost one thousand dollars so far and this includes everything! Now that is a pretty cheap vacation for a family of four! To say the least, we are all having a heck of a good time and just can not believe all the beautiful country up here. Now that the work is finished we are off to hike up Healy Mountain and visit Horseshoe Lake. One thing we can definitely say is the trails here go either straight up or steep down! Either way is quite an exercise in the leg muscles. It was a good day and fun too.

7-4-77 Cont. This evening we went to another mini lecture on mosquitoes which was very good and educational. The park rangers do a very good job with their lectures in the evenings around a nice campfire. After the campfire lecture we headed over to the hotel once again to see what they had to offer for entertainment. We watched another beautiful slide show in the hotel dining room about the flora, fauna and moods of Mount McKinley. Then a lovely walk back to our camp for our nightly cribbage tournament.

7-5-77 After a leisurely breakfast we broke camp, packed the plane up and readied ourselves for a flight north. We sent a bunch of stuff home in the mail this morning, bid our new friends farewell and departed for Nenana to fuel up. Nenana is a very small and about three miles from the airport so we departed immediately for Fairbanks. We walked about eight miles in Fairbanks looking for hot showers and a Laundromat. Finally found a place to shower and do laundry but had to pay a five dollar fee for a campsite which we were not even going to use. By the time we all had showers and washed our dirty clothing it was 9pm. We had many good conversations with people who had driven the ALCAN Highway and are very happy we were able to fly instead of drive. That road can be quite a challenge still today. As a treat we stopped for milkshakes at McDonalds on our way back to the airplane where our tents are pitched under the wings at Phillips Field. Boy, bed felt so good!

7-6-77 We walked into downtown Fairbanks to locate the Post Office so we can get a mail drop from home. While going through several shops we located a bus schedule and bought many tokens as we will use them over time. Then we walked and rode a bus part of the way over to the Riverboat Discovery to take their four hour trip on the Chena and Tanana Rivers in a sternwheel paddle boat. That turned out to be a fantastic trip full of local history and the Athabascan Indian culture. We stopped over on the Tanana River at Howard Luke's, an Athabascan Indian, fish camp and trappers cabin. He showed us how he catches salmon in a fish wheel, dries and smokes them. This is quite a process. He was also working on tanning some hides for materials for clothing. That was the most educational and interesting hands on afternoon of culture.

7-6-77 Cont. The riverboat even served tea and cookies mid way through the trip. Another interesting phenomenon on the trip was the melding of the two rivers where they meet. There is a perfect line where the waters meet as the Chena runs very dark and clear while the Tanana is glacial fed and runs very milking with silt with only the currents and eddies making the line of dark and milky water waver. On our walk back to camp we stopped off at a Safeway store to purchase some groceries. Arrived home, as we call our tents now, about 8pm for our cribbage and cookie session.

7-7-77 We slept a bit late today then walked down to Alaskaland Park where we wandered for many hours through the Gold Rush Town, Mining Camp, Eskimo Village and more. They have a great little pioneer museum and a steam train that circles through the park. There was even a small zoo out in the back corner with only a few of the Alaskan wild animals. Shopped for our dinner ingredients and returned to our camp about 6pm. After dinner we wrote letters to our parents then had our nightly cribbage tournament until midnight. Dick is not feeling to good as he picked up a cold so I gave him some aspirin and orange juice before bedtime.

7-8-77 First thing this morning we took a bus downtown and wandered around some of the shops here. We had to get more money from a bank, mail off our letters, shop for more food which we do almost daily because we do not have cold storage in our camp. We enjoyed looking around the big Penney's department store. We arrived back at our camp around 4:30pm and Dick decided to change oil in the airplane.

7-8-77 cont. Since we are getting rain showers now and then we rigged up a tarp over one wing with the airplane door latched open and the tarp tied to tent stakes off to the side. The inside of the plane serves as a cupboard. Our Coleman cook stove sits on a five gallon oil can under the wing and the tarp prevents rain from falling in the kitchen area. This works quite nicely. So in a good downpour we had a nice dinner and retired to the tent for cribbage.

7-9-77 Saturday again. Boy the time seems to fly by when you are having fun every day! After getting washed up, changing clothes and packing our camp up, we flew out to Lake Minchumina to camp for a few days and look at some land possibilities. This lake is nine miles long by five miles wide and lays about eight miles from the geographic center of Alaska. Sixty-five miles southeast of the lake is Mt. McKinley and you have a lovely view of the Alaskan Range from here. The skies are so clean and clear and fishing seems to be great at this lake. We walked around and visited with some of the local people. There is a cluster of seven small houses, now deserted, that had been an old FAA station. The station is not manned any longer but still works as a repeater for the FAA through McGrath, Alaska. Dick and I set up the tent and went after some fresh water while the boys went fishing in the lake. The runway parallels the lake and you can camp right where you park the plane. As we were coming back with fresh water we saw the boys running toward us with Jeff yelling, "Hey, Mom, I got a fish this big" while holding their hands out about 24 inches apart. Well, Dick and I both laughed so hard and then Robert ran up shouting, "I got three more and now we can have dinner." When we all got back to the airplane we could not believe it as hanging from our prop was 4 huge northern pike fish running 16-24 inches. These were promptly cleaned and cooked for dinner. Wow, were they ever delicious simply grilled on a small fire with salt and pepper! Fishing really is superb here and we found that several charter planes keep quite busy all summer flying in fishermen on the weekends (mostly from Fairbanks). So we had our first "home caught" fish dinner which was great. I will never again tell they boys that they cannot catch more than four fish as we have no way to keep them, it will be size designated from now on. To say the least we were really stuffed that night!

7-9-77 Cont. We celebrated Jeff's first fish caught in Alaska and the biggest so far by having an extra cookie each after cribbage. The boys went swimming for a couple of hours this evening too and seem to have loads of fun.

7-10-77 Sunday. Well, we are into week number four now and all of us still enjoying our great Alaskan adventure trip. We had a lovely breakfast and then hiked over to the Holmes homestead to the north of where we are camped. After visiting with them for a while we found they would like to retire and have the local power plant up for sale along with a few parcels of land along the lake. More than four hours later and several cups of tea we had heard all about the business, building a log home, actual living expenses out here, schooling etc. and getting a grande tour of the whole set up we were ready to buy the place and stay here. To say the least we are very excited right now as this seems to be right up our alley. I could even work part time for NOAA sending in weather reports a few times a day. The boys would be home schooled like the other children out here. This proposition would give us a boat to keep and we could live in a little log cabin until we could build our own house. Gardening is fantastic here and the greenhouse is full of produce. Now all we have to do is sell out everything in Kennedy Meadows and come up with the down payment of $31, 380.00. This place sits about 150 miles from Fairbanks and 100 miles each from two other small communities. There is a mail and supply plane every Saturday from Fairbanks. One public radio telephone that is located at Holmes' house. Two runways, one with lighting system and a contract to keep the runways cleared and graded.

It is a beautiful location and opportunity for us. Now we wait to see just what happens. The guys are off fishing for our dinner so I walked down the spit to see how they are doing. Robert had two large pike already. I sat and watched Mt. McKinley change in the evening light and that is really lovely. After dinner we had our cribbage games and bedded down in the daylight still at 12:30am.

7-11-77 Well this is sure a very busy lake as there are planes and people in and out, all over the place at all hours of the day and night. We love the setting but are finding it is a bit busy for us. Oh, the tiniest flies here in the millions too! They get into everything and we even have to drink our tea through a head net to filter the flies out. The only time we are without head nets is in our tent. We swam in the lake today which was quite refreshing and felt so good. Dick and the boys did some fishing again while I read some. It has been a very beautiful leisurely day. Dick and I still hold the lead in our cribbage tourney!

7-12-77 This morning we packed up our camp and headed back to Fairbanks with a stop at Manley Hot Springs on our way. It seems to get so much easier and quicker to pack up and load the plane now. As soon as we got to Fairbanks we headed for the post office. Oh, what fun we had reading our mail while sitting right out there on the courthouse steps downtown. Dick and I headed off to the supermarket while the boys stayed at Alaskaland Park to play around. The Dick and I walked back to camp with the groceries and got all our dirty clothes from camp and headed back to meet the boys at Alaskaland. We ate a nice picnic dinner in Alaskaland before heading over to the laundry place for showers and laundry. We arrived back at our camp at 1:30am and went right to bed. Gads, it is so easy to just keep going as the sun shines all the time. I wonder if people sleep forever in the winter time when it is dark more?

7-13-77 After slowly getting things packed up and loaded into the plane we flew to Circle Hot Springs which is a beautiful little old community that is being renovated and under new management. The hotel was really something to see. Then we flew on to Fort Yukon, the largest Indian village in the north, which sits right on the Yukon River. We are now into the land of no roads. We took a lovely walking tour of the town and visited the museum. This town is all old log houses with only a few new wood frame structures. It is totally Indian run under their rules.

7-13-77 Cont. It seems funny to see TV antennas and hear stereos playing at these most primitive homes. The community has a single fresh water supply and most homes have outhouses. Instead of horses and dog sleds like in the old days, everyone now sports a Honda motorcycle or three-wheeler and a snowmobile. You see very few sled dog teams any more. The people are very nice and mostly friendly. We always go to the General Store to visit with local people and to compare prices while shopping for lunch or dinner. Prices are really not as outrageous as everyone has said. Later we flew on to Bettles Field and set up camp for the night.

7-14-77 Bettles is called the hub of the north or the last outpost so to speak. Everything comes through here for delivery to all the northern interior native villages. There is a lodge, post office, trading post, fuel, school and FAA facilities. We are told there is about 70 year round residents with a couple of hundred extras during the summer season due to BLM and geo-surveyors jobs. Up the Koyukuk River about a mile is an Indian Village called Evansville which we at first thought was all part of this same community. We took a walking tour and visited with some of the locals along the way. The boys went fishing in the river which runs alongside the village. The caught grayling, a type of trout, and ate them for lunch. Dick and I met a couple who were fantastic, Bill and Lil Fickus. After a good chat we were invited to fly out to their homestead about 40 miles upriver from Bettles. You talk about a dream place, well that is it! They have lived there for fourteen years and have four children, Girl 17, Matt 15, Linda 12 and Tim 10. Their homestead consists of 160 acres with three fields (wheat, oats and hay), a huge garden with green house, large barn, chicken house, cache, and a two story log house. The John River runs along one side of the homestead and they have a 2200 foot runway on the other side. They have six horses for use in hunting and fun. These are really beautiful people and so friendly to share in their lifestyle with us. Their children loved having company and our boys had a great time with them too. They own a Cessna 180 and another smaller plane, a large CAT tractor and smaller tractor, a flatbed truck and a jeep. In an outbuilding they have a large diesel generator that runs continuously for their power. They are so self sufficient.

7-14-77 Cont. Bill traps in the winter for the furs and meat, guides hunters in the fall in the Brooks Range and flies freight during the summer for other homesteaders. Actually he will do anything to make a living for the family and be able to stay in the wilderness. We really loved their home and plan on going back there to camp for a couple of days next week.

7-15-77 Today we flew over the north slope of the Brooks Range to Umiat to get fuel and on to the northern most town in America, Barrow. You just cannot imagine the flat barrenness of the arctic tundra covered with a million lakes and then all that ocean ice just off shore. It is so awesomely beautiful. Sure hope all our pictures turn out. Barrow is a huge Eskimo village of about 2000 people on the tip of land out in the Arctic Ocean. The wind always blows here, sometimes harder than others, much like Inyokern. The temperatures were warm today at about 35 degrees with a 15-20 knot wind making us wear heavy jackets! These people wear the most beautiful, colorful clothing. It is such a contrast to the stark environment. We proceeded to take a walking tour of the town and visited the shopping center. The boys thought the town looked like a dump but up here everyone hangs onto everything they have ever owned and it is just stacked in the yard when it is no longer useful. Different culture for sure. The fresh water and sewage are a real problem here due to the permafrost. They have big trucks that deliver to the homes fresh water and other trucks that pick up sewage daily. I never learned just what they do with all that sewage later—probably dump it in the ocean! On our walk the boys spotted a nice iceberg that was beached on the shore so they wanted to climb it. Now that made a good photo. This is the only place we have seen so far that I would not want to live as there are no hills, no trees and it is mostly frozen year round. Today was a real test in navigation as ones compass in the plane is not accurate in the far north.

7-15-77 Cont. Trying to read the ground was most difficult with the millions of lakes all looking the same at times. We had to make a stop at Umiat for fuel again and thought we would get a hot cup of coffee and snack in the lodge. Well, I was told it would be $15.00 each as they only sell complete meals so we decided to forget having anything there and just purchased fuel at an ungodly price. We arrived back in Bettles about 9pm.

7-16-77 Today was a day of rest as we recuperated from yesterday's experience. That was a great day but quite stressful at times when flying in the arctic. We all slept until 10am, had our breakfast and cleaned up the camp. Then we wandered over to the lodge to sit around in front with all the locals just talking. The boys went down to the river and spent the day with several Indian kids playing and fishing. This was a very relaxing day. We were invited to a party that the locals were having tonight but we only stayed for a few minutes. There was a lot of very loud music and tons of booze. We each had a coke and went back to our tent for some cribbage.

7-17-77 After breakfast we packed up and checked with the local FSS on the weather before filing a flight plan for four days. Then we flew up the Koyukuk River to Pollacks Bar, a gravel bar at the junction of the north and middle forks of the Koyukuk. It is a beautiful spot for camping and fishing that the locals had told us about. It is about 20 miles out of Bettles. We set up our camp, took baths in the river, had a nice dinner and then took a walk around the bar. We found some fresh bear (mom and baby) and moose tracks. The boys started to drag in dead logs for making a raft. Dick and I watched while having some tea. Eventually we all retired to the tent for cribbage.

7-18-77 This morning we took a lovely hike about a couple of miles up the river. This is sure beautiful country with lots of wild flowers in bloom, fresh animal tracks, big fish and many small creeks which we crossed without taking our boots off. We only got wet to the knees. The peace, quiet and beauty of our surroundings is all so overwhelming and serene. We all love it here. The boys finally finished their raft and we had a launching party. Jeff stayed afloat on it too! What fun the boys are having together! Dick went off to fish for a while. I am going to do some writing. Dick brought back a couple of nice grayling fish which we had with our dinner. Then we all took a walk down river and played games with the boys. Finally we had our cribbage game, cookies and off to bed.

7-19-77 Today was very productive work wise. After breakfast Dick and the boys took a swim while I gathered up our laundry. I washed the clothes down by the river side and the guys made me a nice long clothes line using a wing strut of the plane to tie off to and then using pieces of drift wood to hold up the middle and ends of the line. The boys also got busy constructing a nice log table and four chairs from drift wood. It was fun to sit at our table out on the gravel bar to eat our lunch. The boys called it "KayD's country kitchen". You can not believe how nice it looks and how very comfortable it is. We then walked over to the river junction and watched the boys swim across the very fast current. This is quite difficult to do in the extreme coldness of the water and the swift current even though the river is only about 200 feet across right there. Jeff almost couldn't make it but we all cheered him on and he did it by himself! At least now he knows his limits on swimming in the north country. We played jump rope for a while and then some baseball using a stick bat and rocks for a ball. We had a fun day in the sunshine all by ourselves. Tonight we had our cribbage game outside on our new table and chairs as the mosquitoes were not bad on the gravel bar. We seem to get little thunder showers each afternoon to keep things watered down some.

7-20-77 We had just finished cleaning up our camp after breakfast when a "Super Cub" plane came in and landed on our bar from Bettles.

7-20-77 The pilot Chris, is the local fish and game warden, and he was dropping off his wife, Lynn and all her gear. Chris then returned to Bettles to get Lynn's mother and their kayak. Lynn and her mother, who is visiting from New Jersey, will kayak back to Bettles which is about 30 miles, taking two days to do so. We watched them put the boat together and load all the camp gear on. Then the three had lunch together before the two gals departed in the kayak. Chris stayed with us about an hour or so just chatting. I think he wanted to give the gals time to get down river a bit and then check on them from the air. They are a really neat couple and they even knew Molly McCammon and Wilber. It sure tried to storm good in the late afternoon. The winds came up and sand blew everywhere, the skies turned very black and ominous with thunder rolling. We only wound up with some light showers right here. It sure cooled things down though. We finished off another lovely day with baths in the river, a good dinner followed by our cribbage tournament.

7-21-77 We packed up our camp today and flew back to Bettles for fuel. We had planned to go out to the Fickus homestead but heard they had gone into the city of Fairbanks for some shopping. So we went on back to Fairbanks where the boys stayed at Alaskaland while Dick and I walked into town to pick up our mail. Boy, there was a lot of letters today, which we all enjoyed! We purchased some groceries, did our laundry and went out for dinner at Shakey's Pizza Parlor. There we met a young couple, Jim and Shirley, who gave us a ride back to our camp at the airport with our loaded down backpacks. They invited us over to their trailer house to see some movies of a friend that had surgery with hands only, no instruments! Well, we sure contemplated this and did not believe it. Anyway, we got back to our plane around 11:30pm after a very interesting and thought provoking evening. Played our cribbage and went to bed.

7-22-77 As we were out walking around the airport grounds a local man stopped us to tell us about some very interesting hot springs. We wondered if we had a sign on our foreheads saying we love hot springs! Anyway, we wrote down the information and decided to go have a look. So we packed up and flew out looking for the Melozitna River which is a small tributary to the Yukon. Anyway, we found the hot springs and lodge. We had given a multi day flight plan to the FAA which is so neat, really different from the lower 48. The Melozi Hot Springs runway was clearly marked abandoned but we saw people there so we made a couple of passes and decided to land. There is a young couple, Tom and Roz, who are running the lodge for the summer, a man named Pat who is a handyman, and an Exxon group doing some exploration work for Standard Oil. There is a beautiful, relatively new log lodge with 3-4 cabins, a greenhouse, garden, workshop/garage and a large pool under construction. It is very commercialized though. We had a grand tour with Tom as guide and then went back to set up our camp and settle in for the night. They charge $5.00 a day to camp which includes use of the showers and hot tub. We paid but are really spoiled after free camping until now.

7-23-77 Today the boys and Dick went fishing in the river for grayling, catching enough for dinner at 18 inches or longer. They are really delicious too. I wrote letters and post cards while lounging around the lodge. I gave the boys and Dick haircuts today too before we took our showers. They had an old piano in the lodge which Roz played quite beautifully (classical) but it needed tuning badly. Dick volunteered to tune it for them and we found they had an old accordion so we had a great time after dinner tonight making our own entertainment. Robert spotted the first salmon to come up the creek this year and called to all of us to come see. Maybe we will have some fresh salmon one day?

7-25-77 We have enjoyed lounging around reading, writing, playing instruments in the lodge, taking small hikes and fishing. In fact the boys caught a bunch of fish which they soaked in a brine and prepared for the smoker here at the lodge.

7-25-77 Cont. One of the Exxon men was teaching the boys how to smoke fish. It is a very interesting process. We also learned to poach fish (instead of frying) by Philadelphia Paul. Much healthier for us and taste so good. It pours rain every afternoon which caught me today while I was making tortillas for our dinner. Thankfully we had a tarp up hanging from the wing of the plane and I managed to finish without to much mud involved. We have been watching a grizzly mother and cub about one mile up the creek from us. It is so wild out here and beautiful! The Exxon group left today and almost did not get off the runway without an accident. Trying to carry out to many rocks along with their gear and all. This evening was very quiet in the lodge but we enjoyed Pat's pictures and stories which were an eye opener about Alaska and the oil pipeline. We sure like to own Melozi Hot Springs as it could be a great operation with a bit of work.

7-26-77 This morning we packed up our plane and left for Galena on the Yukon and then on to Nome. We liked Nome which is a lovely old gold rush town much like Skagway. The people are really nice. We did our usual walking around the town and visiting the museum before purchasing some groceries and heading out in the plane for a flight to Serpentine Hot Springs. Wow, what a place this is out in the middle of no where about half way between Nome and Kotzebue! It is very nice like Saline Valley only less accessible and no crowds. Most of the people who use this place are Eskimos who come from the island of Shishmaref about 60 miles away on snow machines in the winter. These people have fixed it up some by building a wood duplex building with a workshop in the center.

They come here in the winters only. Each duplex has 4-6 beds with mattresses, a table and benches, wood stove and various storage shelves and clothes racks. The pool is in another small building and built of redwood with an 8x10 foot deck and benches along two sides. There is a long covered hallway connecting the two buildings so one does not have to go out in the winter time. There is the natural hot springs piped into the pool and then another pipe bringing cold water from the creek just outside and you adjust the temperature to suit yourself.. All of this sits among beautiful tundra covered rolling hills full of wild blueberries. Some of the rock formations are really neat in the hills around here.

7-27-77 We spent a lovely day soaking in the hot pool off and on between hikes, reading and checkers games in the lodge. These cabins are equipped with various games, magazines, paperback books and cards for guests to use. So we are enjoying them while we can. This is a beautiful area to hike and we found some great patches of blueberries that we picked at ate until we were stuffed! The wildflowers are in full bloom everywhere and so colorful. One big rock formation looks just like a big city skyline so we call it the New York City rocks. We have found a few small lakes besides for the cold creek that runs along side the duplexes. Late today a helicopter flew in to fuel up, they have a stash of fuel drums here for the summer season. This crew is on contract to the US Energy Commission trying to locate uranium deposits. The men took a break to go soak in the pool for a while before having some tea with us. We had a fun time chatting with them as they were very interesting fellows. All too soon they were back in the air. We had our nightly cribbage and bedded down for the night indoors.

7-28-77 We spent another glorious day just like yesterday. The weather is beautiful too. We saw many fresh moose and reindeer tracks and droppings on our hikes. The berries are so delicious we keep busy picking them for fresh fruit (blueberries, blackberries and cranberries so far). We never seem to get back to camp with any berries in the bucket but we sure arrive stuffed. Around 9pm a large army Chinook helicopter came in with barrels of fuel for a BLM summer fire camp.

7-28-77 Cont. We gave the crew a tour of the hot springs which surprised them to find so many conveniences out here. The soon left to go to Shishmaref where they picked up a fire crew that would be stationed at the hot springs for the summer. There have been numerous lightening fires, forty-two to date, which are really creating havoc in the interior. You can not imagine how bad the tundra fires can be with the visibility dropping to almost nothing! Tundra seems to smoke and smolder more than actual burning. About midnight the helicopter arrived back here with 32 Eskimos from Shishmaref and 2 white men who were BLM employees. We quickly got dressed and introduced ourselves before sitting around for a couple of hours talking. Eskimos are really fun people as they are always so happy and friendly. It was funny how the men all went off and used the hot tub for a bit and then the women were allowed to do the same. There was no intermingling between the sexes. Now we have 38 people bedding down and sharing two rooms for the night. Dick, myself and the two boys all slept on one twin size bed by having two with our heads at each end and all the feet coming together in the middle. It was fun to listen to the Eskimos argue over who would get the caribou hides to sleep with on floor. with. It seems that the hides were the most popular item around.

7-29-77 After breakfast this morning we all joined together to get the cleaning chores done and bring in some fresh water for the duplexes. During this time we learned a lot about Eskimos as they shared stories with us about how they live, their education, ways of having fun in the wilderness and so much more. One of our new friends is the oldest reindeer herder, Chester, and another is Herbert Nayukpuk, a famous ivory carver from Shishmaref. We were having a lot of fun with these people. It was decided by the elders that a new outhouse hole needed to be dug and so our boys joined in the work party to get the job done. I went off with many of the women to show them were all the berries were as most of them had never been here in the summer, only in the winter time. We had fun picking, singing and just enjoying the sunshine. The camp was really crowded and since we were only visitors we chose to move on. So we packed up our plane and left about 1pm for Kotzebue. Kotzebue is a charming Eskimo village with the runway in the middle of a lake but built up with gravel. We took our walking tour of town and visited the museum. Then we found a store to purchase some groceries and mailed off some letters before walking back out to the airport. While in town we saw a very good Eskimo dancer, Paul Green, perform and bought a book about him. Also found a book about Chester and a tiny cookbook for Eskimos. Dick bought me a pendant and bracelet that is etched fossilized ivory and made by Herbert Nayukpuk which makes it very special to us. The bracelet etchings tell a story. They are very pretty. Due to all the fires burning in the area the visibility was quite poor but we departed for Ambler which lies along the Kobuk River. We had to follow the river all the way to the small community so we wouldn't get lost. We even flew by the Kobuk Sand Dunes which are huge and never saw them through all the smoke. Boy, were we ever tired by the time we reached Ambler. Most of the community are out fire fighting so it was very quiet about the village. We took a walking tour of town which has about a 200 population year round. There are more dog teams than anyplace we have been to so far. We finally met a couple of fellows working construction on a new airport and roadway and went to their cabin to get some fresh water. We then pitched our tent under the wing and went to bed exhausted.

7-30-77 After breakfast we took a walk down to the waterfront where we met Mark Cleveland, owner of one of the general stores. I made the mistake of asking him immediately if he had any fresh meat for sale and he told me the store is closed. I did not know what I had done to upset him but he absolutely refused to serve us then. After meeting several other natives in the village I was able to learn that I had been very rude.

7-30-78 Cont. Doing business with the natives is a very slow and talkative process where one discusses the weather, fishing/hunting and other items of interest before getting down to business. I had not taken any time before asking questions? Oh well, I won't make that mistake again! I even went back and talked with Mark later and apologized for being rude. We then had a nice conversation. During our wandering we met a man, Dave Rue, who has Ambler Air Service who was quite charming and we talked for a long time about life and flying in the bush of Alaska. We did locate some fresh meat out near the back of town at a woman's cabin and bought a pound of ground meat. We packed up our camp as we were ready to move on to the Ambler River to visit with Molly McCammon and Wilbur. Then we found out that they had gone into Kotzebue to get their new "powered canoe" and would be awhile until they returned home. We left them a note on a pile of their supplies at Ambler and headed off to find their cabin. We had a good flight and found their cabin quite easy but the river had changed and the sand bars were not long enough for us to land and get off again fully loaded. We could have landed but not taken off with our almost overloaded plane. It was very disappointing to only be able to fly around and take some pictures but we had to fly on to Bettles before running to low on fuel. At Bettles we fueled the plane, went into the lodge for ice cream and soda for a special treat before flying on up river to our lovely gravel bar campsite. We saw moose on a lake and took some pictures. They are huge animals.

7-31-77 HAPPY ANNIVERSARY (our 16th) for us! We had a lovely day walking, fishing, swimming and playing water Frisbee with our gold pan. I have been reading our new Alaska books out loud for about one hour each evening. This is a beautiful way to relax and we are learning a lot at the same time. Dick and the boys watched two bears fishing in the river about 1000 feet up stream of our camp. Fascinating! We all walked back to that area after dinner but no more bears, only their tracks. I really wanted to see them too. We are still having our fun cribbage tournaments before bedtime but the boys are getting much better at playing and really give us a battle to hold the lead.

8-1-77 Today we all went along the river trying our hand at some gold panning with only a few tiny flakes. We actually found it was more fun to play water Frisbee with the pan with each of us taking a stand out in the water forming a diamond shape and we toss the pan across to each other. In fact we were enjoying this game and of course, we were all nude when around the corner from the middle fork of the river comes a canoe with a couple in it. I said to Dick, "Oh my, now what do I do?" He said it is too late to do anything so just wave and say hello! That couple was very nice and even thought we were having more fun than they were. I finally got out of the water dressed and spent the afternoon doing our laundry. We had another good swim later then back to our country kitchen for some reading and playing cribbage. Now this is what I call a relaxing vacation and great fun!

8-2-77 The visibility was only about one quarter of a mile all day. The air felt very heavy. We did see three planes just off the water and two canoes full of people on their way to Bettles, about 30 miles down stream. We finished reading our Alaska books today. Then I wrote some letters, cards and paid bills once again to get mailed as soon as we find a post office. After wearing a lot of mosquito repellant all the time we do enjoy having a river where we can jump in and wash up each evening.

8-3-77 This morning we packed up and flew off to Bettles where we fueled the plane, went into the lodge for a coke and to have a last chat with our many new friends there. After all the goodbyes we headed off to Fairbanks. The boys once again chose to stay over at Alaskaland while Dick and I walked into downtown to check our mail, shop and do the laundry for the last time here.

8-3-77 Cont. I called my mother in Inyokern to let her know we are going to start south tomorrow. Do not send any more mail to us. We all arrived back at the plane in early evening where we had a delicious steak dinner to celebrate. Then the usual game and bedtime.

8-4-77 We packed up the plane and made one last trip to the Post Office. The boys and Dick each bought beautiful Alaska leather belts for souvenirs. We are planning on flying down the Alcan Highway with a side trip at first over to Dawson City, Yukon Territory. Oh there are so many miles of the same type of wilderness that it just boggles the mind! Dawson is a lovely town very much like Skagway with all the old turn of the century buildings, wood walkways, dirt streets and saloons. We took a taxi ($3/person) from the airport which is eleven miles out of town to start our walking tour of the town. Even saw a small cabin where Robert Service lived. There are many miles of tailings piled along the Klondike River left in ridges by the gold dredges. It looks like some science fiction landscape with the circular ridges of gravel and such. We had to laugh as we did not spend any money in casinos here but we spent $36 just on the taxi to and from the airport and a light lunch. We are camped out under our wing for the night.

8-5-77 We left Dawson headed for Whitehorse, YT where we were surprised at the size of the city. It is quite large and very modern and is the hub of the Canadian northwest country. This town sits along the beginning of the Yukon River and has a lot of history about the gold rush days. We seem to have spent more time wandering around this town and were getting tired so we found a mini bus that goes to the airport and caught a ride back saving us about a seven mile walk. There was a lot a activity at the airport because a brand new Cessna 180 had crashed on the runway. It sure would be interesting to know what happened there. We have been seeing many Cessna 170's today and all are headed the same direction as us. Almost seems like they had some sort of club fly-in. As soon as we could we departed for Watson Lake where we had a lovely spot to camp right on the grass with trees and the lake alongside. It wasn't long before a Cessna 170B pulled in and camped right by us tonight. The two men were from Michigan.

8-6-77 We packed up our plane and headed over to the fuel pumps where we met two more Cessna 170's waiting for fuel. It was more than thirty minutes before we could fuel due to a power outage so we all had a grand time visiting and getting to know one another. One of the planes had two men from Big Bear Lake, CA and they even knew my dad. It is a small world out here. The other plane had a couple from Anchorage, he is an air traffic controller going on vacation. We found out about a Cessna 170 convention going on in Edmonton, Ontario, which explains all the 170's we have been seeing going south. They are sure all neat people. Well, we finally got fueled and flew off for Fort Nelson, BC for a fuel stop again. Then we flew on to Fort St. John where we set up camp for the night. This is a beautiful farming area surrounded by wilderness with a lot of gas/oil productions (the main industry) going on. We see that land here runs from $50/acre to $400/acre near town. There are a lot of logging operations and pulp mills which smell.

8-7-77 We departed early for Prince George where we ate lunch and then flew on to Williams Lake to camp for the night. We are still seeing so much beautiful country and even crossed the Canadian Rockies today. It is nice to see some high altitudes again. Today will mark our departure from Canada and we figure the conclusion of our trip to the far north country. To say it has been spectacular is putting it mildly! We are all so very thankful we had the time and proper equipment for making such an incredible journey. I think this trip will stay in our hearts forever.

8-8-77 Today we flew into Bellingham, WA to clear customs back into the USA. It was sort of sad to have our journey coming to an end but we are all hoping to one day move up to Alaska and make it our home. The rest of the trip over the next three days was sort of a repeat of the beginning. We arrived home without incident and were greeted by many friends.

Our Beginning — 1960

1960 - Dick in Japan

Kay's Senior year - 1960 High School

1961 - Our wedding day

1962 - Shortly before our first son's birth

Kennedy Meadows, California

Nine mile canyon road from 2400 feet at desert floor to Chimney Peak at 6000 feet with cool pine scented forest. Then on to Kennedy Meadows over a 7500 foot pass was part of our daily commute to work.

Our first hand built cabin — A-Frame with loft, 12x12 feet at floor in Kennedy Meadows.

1963 — Dick, Kay and son Robert.

1964-1965 — Dick working on our first house which was built without power tools.

1966 — The windmill that pumped water from our hand dug well.

Our house on top of a knoll — unfinished but we live in it. Dick, Kay, 2 friends, our sons and dog.

The view from kitchen window over our rock terraced patio across Kennedy Meadows. See the 4 foot diameter slab of tree mounted on round of wood that was our picnic table.

1964 — Our son Jeff in cabin with 15 gallon water crock and bookshelf cupboards in background.

View of our house from across the subdivision all nestled in piñon pine trees. Windmill barely visible to left of house.

1965 — Our sons in unfinished house with tar papered window.

Robert and Jeff rode their burros many miles over the years having fun.

Family picnic with Dick's mother to Monache Meadow's.

1961 — Dick's parents
Norton and Betty Johnson.

Their home in Reseda, CA

Kay's Mom (Mary) and Les Hill
in Inyokern, California

Mary and Les Hill's wedding in Inyokern Park
Kay Johnson (Maid of honor) and
Ken Hill (best man)

Our Long Lasting Friends and Neighbors

Pauline and Jack Horton

from Neighboring ranches. Kennedy Meadows, California

Joni and Don McCarthy

Jeanette and Bill Riffle

KayD "Healthy breakfast with Jack and Pauline"

Left to right — Friends from Ventura, CA, Pauline, Jack and Dick
KayD and Joni's new guitar case (made by friends of Dick and KayD)

Some favorite desert spots to fly in and explore.

Our sons in camp at Death Valley, California where the temperature dropped to 19˚f that night.

Then make music around the campfire. Kay and son, Jeff.

Our grandchildren sharing fun at Amanda's house.
Amanda, Crystalynn and Jeffrey

Annual K.M.V.F.D. barbecue fund raiser to build up a volunteer fire department.

Another way to explore riding a mechanical mule with long time friend Bob Weinhardt.

Alaska — 1979 to Present

Our friends
Don and Alice Hulshize.
The realtor who helped us settle on the Salcha River.

The beautiful Salcha River.

Our dreamboat launching on Salcha River.

1979 —
Our land
when we
first saw it.
16x16 foot
cabin.

Tiny out house.

Lovely gravel bar
across the river
for a runway.

We added on a 12x24 foot room to cabin for bedrooms.

Unfinished bedroom

China cabinet all hand made with chain saw. Even has glass door on top.

1994-1995 — Building a larger one and a half story house for our retirement years. Construction went on until snow stopped us for the winter.

1996 — Outside of new house completed.

1989 — Putting a water well in shop for our shower room and laundry facilities.

Springtime falling trees, peeling bark off to make logs ready for new construction projects. Then cleaning up debris.

This is where we built our airplane!

The cabin kitchen after rebuild project in 1985.

Our beautiful 550# cast iron stove!

Kay working the hand winch on gin pole to unload a 550 pound cast iron stove from boat.

Dick in boat to hook up and guide lift cable on gin pole winch.
A visiting friend helps hold gin pole to guide load away from boat top.

Wild life viewing right in our yard.

Cow and calf moose.

A cross-fox that came everyday to eat and play.
"Miss Foxy"

Or just sitting on our serenity deck by the riverside to watch the water flow and grass grow.
Our favorite pastimes.

Our gravel bar runway from airplane view. Our cabin sits in the trees on left side of river

Our original riverboat with homemade windshield and canvas top.

Our first snow machine on runway across from our cabin. Dick driving, me sitting on sled and son, Jeff riding on back of sled. Temperature 20 below zero F.

Various times of break-up — when the ice goes out in spring time.

OOPS! Should keep rubber side down.

Our old double-wide snow machine after rolling off 6 foot river bank.
Thankfully the roll bar saved Dick's life.

Riverflow is constantly changing the river course.

Aerial view of our runway in early winter.

Lower gravel bar runway is gone.

New gravel bar growing on our cabin side of the river.

Landed our Cessna 170 to give it a good washing.

1993 — Our new home built aircraft being transported into town for final F.A.A. inspection.

1994 — Winter flying our Kitfox IV plane on skiis was great fun. Dick is all smiles.

The Salcha River Lodge — At the highway has been a big part of our life over the years and many owners.

Our airplane getting fuel at the pumps.

During the years in Fairbanks we maintained a tie down right off the gravel runway for general aviation at the international airport.

Dick commuted by airplane daily.

Flood water in August was 3 feet deep in our yard.

1992 — High water floated firewood around our yard. Dick wading as he secured items around the shop.

Playing piano rolls and singing were a big part of our daily lives.

Occasionally I would play the accordian for fun.

There was always a lot of laughter with our grandchildren when they visited.

Jeffery, Jeff and Crystalynn

Fourth of July barbecues with neighbors each year were fun for all ages.

A picnic lunch from McDonalds with Dick's mom during one of our flyin visits to georgia. Mom's favorite food!

Solar panels gave us electricity from 1983 by keeping our house battery bank charged.

Gathering our food is fun and time consuming...

Dick with a nice string of Grayling fish from our Salcha River.

Dick and Kay dipnetting for Salmon on the Copper River. Nice load of Salmon fill the bow on our boat.

In the fall we hunt moose and caribou which are hung to age in the cool shop. Then we butcher, wrap and freeze, or can in all the meat in pint jars.

Berry picking and preserving cover late July through September.

We harvest from the garden all Summer long.
Canning the remaining vegetables in the Fall.

Nothing like a good wood fired hot tub after a day of hard work.

Father and sons having fun in our shop.

Bob Dick Jeff

Then working together on firewood gathering.

Our son, Bob, drove his motorcycle from Washington with his son, Jeffery, as a passenger for a fun visit to Alaska.

Our sailboat in the Caribbean during our 5 year world adventure. 1997-2002.

We wrote a book of "Our Journals From Crusing The World on the S/V Mermaid."

Available through Dick and KayD Johnson —
Tel: 1 (907) 388-7022
email: dickandkayd907@yahoo.com

500 pages of excitement at sea and shore in exotic ports. With many color photos.

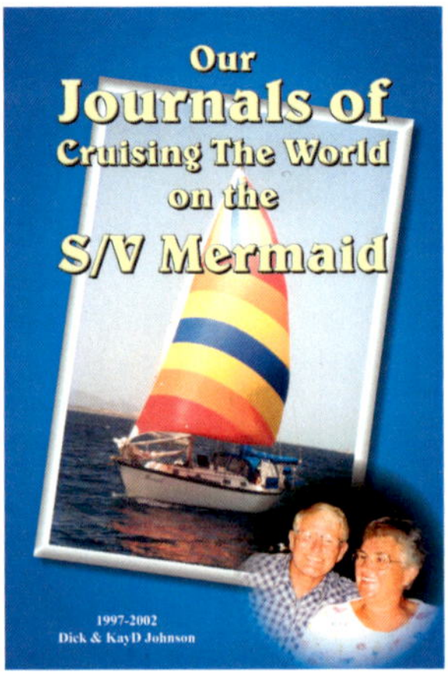

At San Diego, CA harbor the day of our return to the U.S.A. in 2002. Dick and I on the dock.

Part Two

Chapter 8

THE GREAT MOVE TO ALASKA

After returning to our home in the High Sierras of California after our wonderful 1977 summer adventure trip to Alaska, Dick, me and our sons went back to our normal life but always thinking of Alaska. So one day we held a family meeting around the dining room table and discussed what everyone thought about maybe moving to Alaska and building a log cabin for ourselves. Each of us put our thoughts and concerns into the discussion and a decision was made to "just do it!" Now this sounds simple to tell it, but when one has lived for almost 17 years in one place with the boys attending school in one area with all the same children during this time, it becomes a big move for a family. Our sons were both going to be in high school with the oldest in his senior year by the time we could actually move. So the boys had to be sure this is what they wanted to do as well as us. Otherwise we could just wait until they finished their schooling first. It was a unanimous decision to move to Alaska as soon as possible.

Dick and our friend Bob W. had flown to Alaska again in the summer of 1978 checking out the possibility of us purchasing the power plant out at Lake Minchumina. After much haggling over the rights and machinery with the present owners we decided to not purchase that business. Instead we would try to find a job with the FAA or the University of Alaska out of Fairbanks.

I then wrote to about 21 realtors in the city of Fairbanks to check into the availability of land within a one hundred mile radius of Fairbanks hoping to get a lot of information for us to research. That did not happen. We had only two replies.

Next on the list was to inform our employers that we would be leaving the area within the next year. Dick would actually take a leave of absence after his vacation time was spent just in case we had to return. You know the old adage "never burn your bridges behind you."

One weekend we were having coffee with a few friends at our place talking about selling our home as we planned to move to Alaska. The next thing we knew we had phone calls at work that week wanting to get more information on our house. One couple came up the mountain the next weekend to look at our place and made arrangements to meet us at the bank on the following Monday. Wow, this was a bit fast as we had not even advertised anything at this time. Anyway, we sold the house for exactly what we were asking and we carried the papers ourselves. It was all set up with our bank and we had two months to move out.

We immediately started looking into moving companies but they wanted far too much money for a move to Alaska. That is when we decided to just purchase an old moving van and do it all ourselves. So after a short search we found the ideal van for us for only $3500.00. This would hold our belongings until the school year ended. We would rent a small cabin right off the runway at Horton's ranch where we have been flying off to work daily until school ended as well. Now we know what the plan is and we set to work making it happen. We lived in this small cabin for almost one year.

Then the big move day came……………..

June 16, 1979 Some people say we are having a midlife crisis as Dick just turned 40, we have two teenage sons and we are setting off on a new adventure into the unknown thousands of miles away from our hometown. Dick and I finished loading all our possessions into the small moving van that we purchased one year ago, just after selling our home in Kennedy Meadows. We have spent the past year living in a small cabin over on Horton's Ranch in Kennedy Meadows, California and using the moving van to store most of our household goods in. In preparation for this move we purchased a one year supply of canned and dried foods, lots of ammunition for our guns and anything else we thought would be cheaper down here in Inyokern, California.

Dick has taken a one year leave of absence from his job at China Lake Navy Base just in case we have problems and need to return to California. We have a bit of savings and my small retirement account from the school district so we feel quite at ease with this move. Both of our vehicles, a moving van and a VW van, have been serviced and we are carrying extra spare tires so we are confident that the drive will go well.

The boys and I will be driving to Fairbanks, Alaska alone with our 17 year old son Robert driving the big moving van truck and 15 year old brother Jeff riding shot gun with him. I will drive our VW van which is loaded to the hilt with our camping gear and whatever else we needed to stuff in there. It seems like both vehicles are over loaded. Since the big van is slow we are sticking to back roads and off of the interstate highways. This should make for a very scenic interesting trip.

Dick, who is already a commercial pilot, is signed up for his instrument rating flight school which takes about a week to get certified. Dick will be in Clear Lake, California during this time of training. The school will be quite intensive with days of flight training under a hood, sort of like flying blindfolded since you cannot see out the windows of the plane. We hope to all meet up in about two weeks in Fairbanks, Alaska.

June 17, 1979 So with many hugs all around and a small bit of trepidation on my part we departed Kennedy Meadows after living there for over 17 years. Dick rode in the moving van with our sons to the bottom of the steep nine mile canyon to be sure Robert could handle the truck alright. A neighbor followed and took Dick back to our airplane. One must remember that this is all happening long before cell phones were in use so Dick and I will be totally out of contact during the entire trip. When we finally got down to highway 395 we had a 40 mile per hour head wind as we turned north which is not helping our fuel mileage.

It is now 8pm Sunday here at Taboose Creek, California. The boys and I had stopped here for a short visit with our dear friends the Bentleys and to have our lunch. We left Bentleys about 1:30pm but we did not even get beyond the turn onto highway 395, about one block. Just as I pulled onto the highway the right rear transaxle came loose from the wheel on the VW van. Since it is Sunday I cannot get it fixed so with Bentley's help we pushed the VW back to their yard and stayed at their house overnight. Bob and Billie had an engagement for the evening so the boys and I enjoyed our spaghetti dinner, watched a bit of TV and hit the sack. Right now I am terribly discouraged and I can not even talk to Dick about it. I must buckle up and solve my own problems.

June 18, 1979 At 7:30am we called a tow truck in Big Pine to haul the VW into Bishop to the nearest VW dealer. This cost me $69.50 and we are not far from home yet! Sure hope we are able to get things fixed and be back on the road by noon.

It is now 7:50pm and we are in Reno, Nevada, at a KOA campground. It is hard to believe we left Bishop by 10:15am after a bit of a hassle with the VW dealer there. It seems that nothing was broken on the VW but the bolts were not tightened properly in Ridgecrest when we had it fully serviced and when it fell apart it damaged one small part. Anyway, the Bishop dealer contacted the Ridgecrest dealer where the service had been done and they took care of the repairs but I had to cover the towing. I plan to bill my insurance company and hope like heck they will pay the towing bill. This has not been a good start for a long journey of about 3600 miles from Inyokern, California to Fairbanks, Alaska. After fueling up in Bishop we figured the moving van got about 5mpg and the VW got 12mpg in yesterday's headwinds.
This gives us a good idea on how often we need to fuel the big truck on our long journey. We arrived in Bridgeport at 1:15 pm where we stopped for fuel and lunch. The VW has increased to 20mpg but the heavily loaded moving van is still at 5mpg. There has not been much wind today which is nice so we drove on to Reno where we had a hard time finding a place large enough to fuel up the

moving van. Today's driving has been that part of Highway 395 which is all mountain climbing or descending but quite beautiful as we passed a few lakes and big meadows with the high sierra mountains alongside.

June 19, 1979 We have stopped for the night as it is 6:50pm and we are 20 miles south of Burns, Oregon. We had a very good day and covered over 300 miles. We managed to get started about 8am today and then just kept right on trucking except for quick stops for fuel and lunch. There is so much beautiful country along this route with an occasional ranch. We have not encountered any fuel problems after leaving Reno. We stopped at "Jerry's" in Alturas for lunch (much like Denney's restaurants) today just for fun. I think we are all missing Richard very much since we have always been together for every trip in our lives.

June 20, 1979 It is 10 pm and we are in Spokane, WA. I am waiting for our clothes to dry at this KOA campground laundry. After 14 hours on the road today we took hot showers and cleaned up which felt so very good. The boys went swimming while I did the laundry. The moving van is doing just fine so we took the speed limit up to 45 mph to try and cover more ground because we have lost a day already. Today we managed 410 miles which is about 110 miles too many as it was exhausting! We are hoping to be in Canada some where near Williams Lake, BC tomorrow. Boy, I really miss Richard but I know I can do this myself and the boys have been just great.

June 21, 1979 We are just outside of Vernon, BC in Canada. We had a beautiful trip today and made 309 miles putting us about two hours north of Williams Lake. The moving van had a flat tire due to a rock in the outside dual wall so we had to stop and get it fixed at Coleville, WA for only $9.50. Then later in the day the VW had a starting problem but the boys are keeping me going.

Canadian Customs was a breeze. They did ask a lot of questions and were not happy about my money situation because they thought I needed to have more cash on me than $600. Robert found the moving van was really overloaded by almost 1500 pounds but the customs gave us an OK because it was all personal household goods. We were questioned about how much food we carried in the VW and I could honestly say about a weeks worth of food in the VW. Thank heaven they did not ask that question about the moving van which had a years supply of canned and dry goods! That was not lying, but just not adding information to the question asked.

June 22, 1979 Quesnel, BC. We traveled 315 miles today. Boy, the country just seems to get prettier and we have even seen it before from our airplane when we flew across this same path in 1977. At one point we had a doe deer run alongside the car for a block or so. We also stopped for a cute duck and her eight little ducklings to cross the road. Today was our first day of rain on the trip.

We met some people from California that are going to Alaska. They came over to our camp to thank us for the lovely music around the campfire as Jeff was playing his banjo and I played the melodica. We are getting anxious to arrive at Milepost 0 at the start of the Alaska Highway. We sure love you and miss you, Richard, and hope your school is going great.

June 23, 1979 It is 8pm and we are at Milepost 0 of the Alaska Highway in Dawson Creek, BC! Well, we are really excited tonight as from here on we are into some great wilderness driving with communities few and far between with lots of sunshine as the days get much longer. All this makes for pleasant driving and fun campfires in the evening during sunlight. There is only about 1500 miles to go to Fairbanks, Alaska. The Alaska Highway is a narrow two lane road with little shoulders and many places are dirt/gravel for quite a distance. Hope our tires hold out on the moving van.

We saw a huge moose on the side of the road eating his lunch. Tomorrow morning I will go grocery shopping at Safeway for our camp and snack foods while driving. We sure haven't taken many pictures as we don't like to stop any more than necessary since we are a very slow caravan. But we did go on to Milepost 0 in downtown Dawson Creek for some photos.

June 24, 1979 Here we are to a Sunday again and we have been on the road for more than a week now. It is 10:22pm and we stopped for the night at mile 300 at Fort Nelson, BC.

Back at Dawson Creek we waited in the parking lot of Safeway this morning for the store to open only to find out that it is closed on Sunday! This was not a good start to the day but we managed to be "on the road again" about 8:30am. It has poured rain all day with only very short spells of let up. This gives a bit more tension to the driving. We had a good 16 miles of "super snot slippery" road giving us some very interesting driving. You talk about muddy and very slick, boy we had it! The Alcan Highway is very much like the old Kennedy Meadows county road before it was paved. It can be very narrow and rough at times but not to bad. We saw a cute bear ambling along side the road today too.

June 25, 1979 It is 7:30pm Monday. We are at Watson Lake, Yukon Territory and setting up camp early for the night. Traveling was good today with the road in good condition. Hooray! There was one time when I looked back to find the boys, as I was in the lead and had lost sight of them, when my right front tire caught in the soft shoulder of the road. The VW van tried to roll over so I steered into the ditch to stop the rolling action. I went down into the ditch and up the other side of the ditch turning to come back onto the road but the mud was so soft that I didn't quite make it all the way up to the roadway. The boys came along and were laughing so hard they had a great time pulling me back onto the road! To say the least, I will be hearing about this one for a long time.

We saw a lot of beautiful stone sheep along the road today too. It did not take us long to get camp set up as we have a real routine now that works great. I start preparing dinner on the camp stove while the boys pitch the tent and open up the sleeping bags. Then we have the dish water heating while we eat and are able to get all the dishes cleaned up and packed away shortly after finishing dinner. All this takes us less than an hour and we are ready for some fun relaxing by a campfire or walking.

While I was writing in this journal Jeff and Robert were working on the VW trying to find out why the starter quit. Maybe they are getting tired of running behind me giving me a push start at each stop! Anyway, Jeff popped up under the VW and hit his head as he hollered, "I hear our airplane!" So Robert and I listened and recognized the sound immediately too. I ran for the VW and the boys gave me a push start so I could get out to the airport which is 7 miles away from here to catch Richard before he may decide to move on.

I just knew that Richard would be camping for the night right where we had in 1977, just off of the runway alongside the lake in the trees, so I drove right out there. You should have seen Richard's face when I drove up and asked if he would like to spend the night with me! All I heard was, "Oh my god, where did you come from?" He jumped out of the plane and we hugged so hard. It was so good to be together again. Dick said he had looked out the window when he heard a car but didn't recognize the muddy VW.

When we arrived back at our campground the boys were playing music and talking to some neighbors from another camp. These people were really shocked to find out that I really had picked up my husband at the airport and we have not been in touch since June 16th. They had so many questions for
us as they were very interested in a family packing up and moving to Alaska. Anyway, we all sat around talking until 12:30am as we had much to catch up on.

Dick and I have decided to meet up each evening from here into Fairbanks so we can share some family camping and be together more. Plus he can help with any problems we get.

June 26, 1979 It is 9:30pm and we are in Whitehorse, Yukon Territory. I must report that we had flat tire number two on the moving van right at Johnson's Crossing. It was an inside dual making it much harder to change but we did manage it all quite well. This made us late getting into Whitehorse by about an hour tonight. We got the camp all set up and I went to the airport to pick up Richard. We are camped alongside the Yukon River near the beginning of it. It sure is more fun having the family all together in the evenings now. It also gives us more incentive to reach a particular destination each day. We saw some bears right along side the road again and stopped to take some photos this time.

Boy, we sure love the long sunshiny days but it makes it hard to go to bed. I think I get much more tired than the boys do but they have each other to talk to and keep laughing all day long. I have been playing cassette tapes to help pass the time as I drive.

June 27, 1979 We made it into Alaska today and are at Northway right along side the runway where it is 10pm and still very sunny out. This has been one heck of a day. First of all, we had our flat truck spare tire fixed before leaving Whitehorse so we had a very late start. The VW still won't start with the starter, the solenoid is shot and we cannot replace it until we reach Fairbanks. So the boys are still giving me a push at each fuel stop, 3-4 times a day, so that I can pop the clutch to start the motor. Sort of like being a part of the Beverly Hillbillies! Later in the day the truck had flat number 3 on the rear inside dual, opposite side from the last flat. So far three of the four rear tires have taken in a rock giving us a flat tire. I guess we really can't complain when we have covered 3400 miles on very rough road for a good part of the way. Tomorrow we should reach Fairbanks!

Dick took us all out to dinner in the Northway Lodge right here at the airport. Sure delicious and no mess to clean up for us. Then we celebrated our arrival in Alaska with a great slice of berry pie and vanilla ice cream. This was the second dinner out since leaving home, for me and the boys.

Oh, the big event of the day happened after our flat tire and only about four miles from where we were to camp at Northway. We had left the main highway and were headed the seven miles into Northway on a very narrow and muddy road when once again I got to close to the right hand edge of the roadway and the soft shoulder grabbed the right front tire taking my VW about half way off the road on a bank. I was leaning at such an angle I thought I might roll over but a small tree was in the right place to keep me upright! Once again the boys came along behind me and laughed like crazy at Mom's poor driving record. They hooked up a tow line and had me back on the road in only a few minutes. I think the twelve to fourteen hour driving days are getting to me and I am making stupid errors. It is pouring rain and has been all afternoon. This gives the dirt roads a nice slick surface. We soon met up with Richard at the airport and the boys just couldn't wait to tell him about pulling Mom out of the ditch again! Richard just laughed at me too and said, "That's twice!" This is an old family joke.

June 28, 1979 It is 5pm Thursday and we are parked on the side of the road about 38 miles south of Delta Junction. Today was going great for awhile and we were all very happy because this would be our last day on the road and this far into the trip we had not had any major problems. That was until 1pm when the truck just flat quit running. The boys and I figured it was a clogged fuel filter or the fuel pump. So I left them with the truck and I drove on toward Delta to try and find either a tow truck or someone who could help us. At a small lodge I found a mechanic who returned with me to the moving van. When I got back to the moving van there was our airplane pushed off the side of the highway with the wings parallel to the roadway so the plane was totally clear of the roadway. Richard was working on the truck. It seems that his departure from Northway had been delayed due to the weather and he was behind us and happened to fly right over the parked truck on the roadside. After circling the truck in the air and checking the highway for traffic Dick proceeded to land on the highway and see what our problem was. The fuel pump was shot and our mechanic friend said the nearest fuel pump for that truck would be in Fairbanks, 138 miles away. So Dick decided to fly off to Fairbanks, get the part and return to us and install it. Wow, are we ever lucky to have a personal fly-in mechanic! So the boys and I are waiting and hopefully we can still make it to Fairbanks tonight.

That would give us a total of 12 days en route over 3604 miles using just under $1000.00 for gas and oil. After getting back on the road again we saw a couple of moose and had to stop for them to get out of the road. Wow, they are really huge animals and seem much bigger than even a horse!

June 29, 1979 Today is Friday, 9pm and we are in Fairbanks, Alaska! Well, we finally made it and are all so happy to be here. Dick had arrived back at the truck last night around 7pm after his trip by plane to get a new fuel pump. After Dick installed the new pump, we headed for Delta Junction and a gas station. We had a problem starting the truck due to a low battery after several attempts to start when we had the bad fuel pump. So we gave up traveling for the night and decided to get a good sleep and head off for the final 100 miles to Fairbanks in the morning. It has poured rain all the way today. After arriving in Fairbanks we found a campground and got the boys settled with the van to set up our camp. By this time it was 10:30am and I went to the airport to pick up Dick. After getting the camp all set up for an extended stay, taking showers, doing the laundry (including all our coats and sleeping bags which smelled like campfires), we went grocery shopping and checked for our mail at General Delivery in the downtown post office.

We tried to apply for a Post Office box but were told we had to have an Alaska ID first. So we proceeded to go by the Department of Motor Vehicles to get an Alaska driver's license and were told we couldn't do that without having an address. Now we are between a rock and a hard spot! No license, no address and can not get one without the other. You talk about a "catch 22" situation. We were told it will be about eight weeks before we can get a Post Office box so in the meantime we will continue on with General Delivery mail at the downtown post office. Next we will try to get a bank account started if we can without all the other ID and address. So we are not official residents yet, darn!

Tomorrow we will actively go to some realtors to start hunting for some property. Dick will job hunt starting on Monday. In the meantime, we have a very nice camp set up with two tents and our bicycles out for traveling around town. The campsite actually covers two places because of the moving van and VW van. I wonder how long we will live here before we find some property to move onto.

We simply must get settled in before winter which doesn't leave much time. I am told that July, August and September then winter hits. Oh well, we knew this was to be quite an adventure when we started. Some of our long time friends think we are having a mid-life crisis because we sold most of our stuff and moved north to the unknown! Dick is 40 years old and we both feel great so this is just the beginning of the rest of our lives.

Chapter 9

SETTLING INTO ALASKA, JULY 1979

We were camped out at the Norlite campground in Fairbanks for about three weeks while we purchased land, obtained our Alaska drivers licenses, received a Post Office box and opened a bank account. It felt real good to now say we are Alaskans, even if we are mighty greenhorns or cheechakos as they say here.

Out of the 21 real estate agencies that we had written to over the past year with our request for land only two replies were received. I do not think they knew just how serious we were about moving north! Dick was headed for Alaska in 1960 when I met him, but we married and settled down in the California High Sierras near the south fork of the Kern River where we learned to live in the wilderness, build a house and spend the next 17 years raising our sons. Anyway, thanks to one very special lady, Alice Hulshizer, who worked for Golden North Realty in Fairbanks, we were soon sent out with her husband, Don, by boat to view three parcels of land on the Salcha River.

What a fantastic experience that was as we had a lovely boat trip for several hours on the Salcha River and found just what we were looking for! It was a five acre parcel with about 400 feet of river frontage that had a small log cabin, 16x16 foot, an outhouse and most important a great gravel bar just across the river from the cabin that would become our runway. Most of the boats on the river at that time were flat bottom open Jon boats with outboard engines. So now we knew what we needed to look for so we could move all our belongings up the river to our new home. We noticed several people had lovely covered inboard jet boats and even some with fancy airboats but those were far to expensive for us at that time. So while we waited for our escrow to close we looked around town for a good boat and outboard motor. Our son, Jeff, found just what we needed for a boat when he was wandering around town with his bicycle and had stopped at Beaver Sports. Then we needed a rack to put on top of the VW van to carry our boat out to the river. At that time we didn't feel like we wanted to spend more money on a boat trailer but we did wind up getting one before the year was over.

Now you can imagine the fun we had as we launched our new 16 foot Alumacraft Jon boat and installed the 40 horsepower Mercury outboard with a jet unit instead of a prop, after building up the transom with plywood first. We had never owned a boat and had no experience in river running but the best way to learn something is just get out and do it! That was our attitude. Thankfully we had already been up the river with Don Hulshizer so we had a preview of where to run.

We had about one week left in July and wanted to get the moving van emptied out so we could put the van up for sale. With our sons taking turns driving the new boat we started our nine day trek hauling two boat loads per day to unload all our things and get them up to the small 16 foot square log cabin. We had been told that our cabin was about 30 miles up the Salcha River and knew it should take us about an hour to get there. Dick would take one son with him for a load while the other son stayed at the cabin with me to help organize all the stuff coming in and clean up a bit of a yard as the bushes and grass were waist high. This gave both boys a lot of boat driving time which they thoroughly enjoyed. The next trip the boys changed places to keep everyone happy and enjoying their jobs. Dick didn't get to drive the boat until our sons finished school and left home!

I realize that this doesn't sound like much of a job but when you consider that our furniture included an 800 pound antique player piano, a 500 pound cast iron wood stove along with many bulky items that had to be unloaded from the high moving van and carried out to be loaded on the boat sitting on the gravel bar upriver just around the corner from the real boat landing. This was the closest we could drive to our new home. Since we were going to be several days in progress moving we did not want to tie up space at the boat landing and get our new neighbors upset with us. Plus we could drive the moving van out onto the gravel bar much closer to the boat which was a great help in the loading process.

When it came time to take the piano there just happened to be a couple of men out on the gravel bar fishing so my husband walked over and asked them if they could lend a hand in loading a piano onto our small boat. They just laughed and said, "You are kidding right?" When they found my husband was very serious they had to admit it was one great story to take home from their fishing trip. This boat trip with the piano took more than three hours because of the heavy load and the boat would not get on step. I was getting quite concerned about the well being of my husband and son after two hours and no sign of them. Later we found that this happened to be the first piano on the river and everyone enjoyed coming by to listen and play some piano rolls.

Then we were busy for many hours unloading the piano and getting it up a six foot high riverbank and several hundred feet back into the woods to the cabin. First thing we did was to take everything possible off of the piano and carry the pieces to the cabin to make the bulk of the piano lighter. Then by using ropes and sheets of 3/4 inch plywood that were 4x8 feet, I was the dead man on the end of the rope and pulled while the three guys pushed so we could maneuver the piano one sheet of plywood at a time up the bank and 125 feet through the woods to the cabin. This was a fairly easy job once we figured it all out and worked as a team. Then we used a pulley and come-a-long to hoist the piano up four feet off the ground to the front porch using the overhanging logs for a base to pull from. We had already used this same system to move the heavy stove but I did not expect it to work so well for the huge piano.

Once we had all our stuff moved up the river I was really busy trying to fit everything into the small cabin. We had two sets of bunk beds against the back wall with a small walk space in front of one set of beds with the piano blocking it off for privacy. These were the boy's beds. We slept in the other bunks along the same back wall which were behind the woodstove which set near the middle of the cabin. When you came in the door you could see the beds along the back wall. The wall to the right was kitchen counter with a propane four burner stovetop and an under the counter small propane refrigerator. We found the refrigerator out under the cabin in a heap of junk left by the previous owner. Dick cleaned the fridge up and found only the electrical portion burnt out so he installed it in the cabin, connected to a propane bottle that was outside and it worked just fine. The wall to the left had our two recliner chairs and an end table between them right under a window. Then between the woodstove and the door was the dining table and chairs. Stuffed everywhere possible was boxes of food, clothing and whatever else we had. It was a very tidy, compact place and you walked in and sat down or went to bed as there wasn't room for wandering around. We did wind up with a lot of stuff that had to be stored under the cabin for a while until we had more room.

We did not have a well so we were drawing water from the river with buckets and boiling it for drinking water. To bath during the summer we just used the river. Then when it started getting colder we had a large steel tub that we placed on the floor in front of the woodstove which took two people to carry out and empty in the yard.

It did not take us long to realize that we were going to need to get busy and add on to the cabin for space to keep the four of us from standing on each other! The boys and Dick started to fall trees and we all worked at hauling them into the yard by hand. Two people on each end of the log with a rope wrapped around the log and over our shoulders to raise the log clear of the ground. Each log had to be hauled 50-100 feet through dense woods. This was a lot of work but we made it fun by singing crazy songs and joking along the way. Like one time when the three guys decided to see if Mom could keep up and started moving fast through the woods. My legs are shorter then theirs and I had a tough time going over the dead falls. We laughed until we cried at such silly antics! Since Jeff was very thin at this time due to a spurt of growth we had given him an old towel to use for a pad on his shoulder to keep the rope from cutting in. Well, the next thing we knew Jeff was standing on a stump with that towel tied around his neck and flowing out behind in the breeze hollering, "Superdude to the rescue!" as he jumped. This made all of us laugh so hard at his craziness but it also made the work a bit more fun too.

Then because it was going into August we had to start peeling the bark off the logs using draw knives. When this job is done in the spring it is quite easy as you only need to make one pass the length of the log with a draw knife, after that by using a shovel you are able to just peel the sappy bark right off the tree in one big piece the full length. Instead we had to peel each log one strip at a time and then roll it to continue the process which takes much longer to complete. It is also very back breaking work as one is bent over straddling the log all the time. We needed quite a few logs cleaned up to build a 12x24 foot addition for our bedroom which was to be across the back of the existing cabin in a tee shape.

Since the boys were the only ones who owned chain saws they were doing a good portion of the work. The boys had purchased their chain saws to cut and sell firewood, when we lived in the High Sierras in California, to get spending money. Dick and I had always cut our firewood with a six foot long hand saw, that had belonged to Dick's grandfather, and had handles on each end (a misery whip as we called it). I also used a bow saw for small trees and branches, squaw wood as I called it, when I was alone. After the guys had cut a couple of trees down we moved the logs into the yard using the method described above.

In the meantime, after we had a good pile of logs cut and moved into the yard to be cleaned up, I would sit on the logs and peel them by the hour as Dick and the boys proceeded to notch each log and stack them into position on the new addition to our cabin. This was quite a job since the floor of the existing cabin is about four feet off the ground so that is where our new walls start. Finally we had about four rounds of logs up and felt like we were getting some place since now one could see the size of the addition, 12x24 foot room. Wow so much room will feel like a castle!

On a couple of afternoons Dick and the boys went across the river and did a bit of clearing of the gravel bar to make a nice 900 foot runway. This meant cutting brush, cleaning off the drift wood and filling in some of the dips with gravel to give a smooth gravel surface. Then we took Dick to the highway so he could drive to town and park the moving van with a FOR SALE sign in the window. Dick flew our plane, a 1950 Cessna 170A, back to our log cabin home and proceeded to land on our new gravel bar runway. What a celebration we had that night as we sat out looking at our airplane just across the river and could see all the progress we had made in the yard and on our new addition to the cabin. We were all feeling very proud of ourselves.

Dick would fly out to Fairbanks almost daily trying to find work but was not having much luck. Strangers were not accepted easily in the town of Fairbanks at that time and since we did not know anybody we did not have local references for him. Dick hunted hard and was really trying to get on with the FAA (Federal Aviation Administration) as an electronics technician or the University of Alaska research departments.

On one of the trips to town when we were trying to sell our moving van we found they had a great program on the local radio called Tradio. You just call in and advertise whatever you are trying to sell and people contact you if interested. Well, this sounded great to us but we did not have a contact phone. So we parked our moving van at the highway edge of the University Center Mall right alongside Airport road with a "For Sale" sign in the window and we sat in the mall by the bank of pay telephones using one phone as our contact. After several hours we had many calls and then two different couples who were moving south came to the mall parking lot to see the truck. Wow, the rush was on as they ran across the parking lot trying to get to us for the purchase! We watched all this through the mall glass doors and laughed. The first man in threw some money at us to hold the van while he went to the bank for the cash to purchase the van. It turned out he was transferring out of the FAA and moving to California with his family. That was funny to us. We wound up selling the van for $500 less than we paid for it and we had one full year of storage for our belongings plus the drive up the Alaska Highway with the van which was a great deal for us. To say the least, we were quite happy to get rid of it so easy and so was the buyer for finding such a good deal. You can't beat that!

On that last trip to town to sell the van we had a bit of a problem. As we were taking off from our gravel bar, which was always a minimum short field take off, our tail wheel struck a prone log off the end of the runway and broke the tail wheel spring. Since we could not see the tail wheel from inside the plane we had no idea of any damage but just for safety Dick made a lovely main wheels landing and slowly rolled to a stop to put the tail wheel down. Much to our surprise we still had a tail wheel. So after selling the van and doing a bit of shopping Dick and I were off to the airport to try to fix the airplane tail wheel problem. We always carried a spare spring so it was just a matter of jacking the plane up and replacing the broken spring. We never even thought of what the boys were thinking as they watched us depart for town but they told us later that we caused quite a stir of dirt and sand flying along with a loud pop when the wheel assembly came up and hit the rudder. The boys were just hoping that we would be able to safely land in town and return to the cabin. Gads, those poor boys sometimes went through a lot of worry over their parents!

Well, you have never seen a happier family than us about now as we have all our things moved up river, the moving van sold and we still have over two months to get ready for the winter! The small 16x16 foot cabin was quite crowded but nicely arranged and we all spent very little time inside so the adjustment was easy.

The boys were taking time out to fish regularly keeping us in a good supply of grayling which we ate a lot of. Sometimes when we were working one of the boys would say, "I hear a fish calling and the guys would all run to the boat with their fishing poles to see who would catch the first fish of the day. They always challenged each other for the first fish, the largest fish and the most caught each day. Fun and cheap entertainment for them!

Dick was flying off to town several times a week trying to find a job. On the other days he worked with us as we cut more trees, peeled logs and brought them in to the yard to build an addition of 12x24 foot across the back of the existing cabin. The unused portions of the trees were cut up for firewood.

We figured we had about enough logs to make that addition to the cabin into two bedrooms with a small potty room on the side with a "honey bucket" that we would empty into the outhouse each day. Boy that would make us quite comfy not having to go to the outhouse at night!

The boys were getting to be quite handy with their chain saws. In fact they had cut and built a 4x50 foot log bridge to walk across the small wet dip in the front yard. The boys loved to put our metal bath tub out on the bridge to take their baths in the afternoons. We all worked together clearing brush, cleaning logs for the addition and just trying to make some order of our new home. We worked hard, ate well and yet still had time to play games in the evenings. The extra long daylight was to our advantage.

By now the wild berries were ripening and we took time out to pick a lot of raspberries and blueberries. Later I found the high bush cranberries would make some delicious jams, syrups and even wine. It was so much fun learning to use all the local wild foods. We had purchased some books from the University Co-operative to help us learn about Alaska. Some of the titles were HOW TO BUILD A LOG CABIN IN ALASKA; ALASKA'S WILD MUSHROOMS; ALASKA WILDBERRIES AND COOKING GUIDE; ALASKA AND YUKON WILDFLOWERS GUIDE; GUIDE TO BIRDS OF ALASKA; and ALASKA ALMANAC. Every time we spotted a new plant, flower, berry, bird or fish we researched it to identify and learn about each one. This turned out to be quite fun for all of us.

Since the property did not have a well for water we were using buckets to fetch water from the river, about 125 feet from the cabin door. I would boil all the drinking water to be sure we didn't pick up anything we didn't have when we came here! The cooking and washing water didn't need to be boiled beforehand because it was hot when you used it.

To do the laundry I would set up two metal laundry tubs out on the river bank in the sun and using a scrub board and a clothes washer/plunger the clothes and linens would get very clean. The hardest part was hand wringing the clothes and bedding. Then we had some cable we strung between the trees that I hung the laundry on to dry, laundry air dried smells so fresh. I still had my old wringer washing machine that was stored under the cabin but couldn't use it until we got a generator. We were a few years getting all that set up. So we stayed with the good old fashioned tubs and wash board. It was not bad except for the bed sheets and heavy blue jeans but the boys helped by wringing them out for me.

I hope you don't think that it was all work and no play because we did take time quite often to just fish or picnic. Our neighbors along the river invited us to barbecues and other fun times over the long three day weekends. Our evenings were filled with us playing games a lot and getting into our Cribbage challenges. The boys made various powered boats and things to play with on the small pond out back. I always had knitting projects going on to keep us all in wool socks, hats, mittens and sweaters.

By now Dick was beginning to get a bit depressed as he was not getting hired for work in town. Our money was dwindling and we had made a promise to each other that when we were down to $2000 cash and still no job we would return to California for the winter. So much to the disappointment of all of us we packed up only a few personal things because WE WERE COMING BACK TO SALCHA and we headed out over the first weekend in September 1979. Dick and Robert would drive our VW bus south to Ridgecrest, California. I would fly our Cessna 170 airplane south and Jeff would come with me. We all were so sad to have to head south but sometimes things happen that we cannot help. Trying to get settled into Alaska has been fun but a tough struggle as well.

Jeff and I had a good flight south over about five days. Jeff practiced his navigation with the charts. When we landed in

Inyokern, California I telephoned my mother and asked her what her plans were for dinner tonight. Mom asked me why and I said because I thought we might join her since we just flew in to town. Mom let out a scream and hung up the phone on me. I was laughing so hard and telling Jeff about the call when Mom came speeding into the parking lot with horn honking! Boy, she was lucky not to have a speeding ticket on that run! Mom proceeded to grab me in a big hug and Jeff too. Then she asked where Dick and Robert were. When I told her they may be here in a few days because they were driving the VW, she did not believe me. She went to look in the main hangar and ask everyone there if they saw Dick and Robert. Then it finally sunk in that I was serious and had just flown our airplane down from Alaska by myself and Mom started crying. I laughed and told her that tears were too late because I was already here and she had no worries. Besides I had my 15 year old son with me so I was not alone! My poor mother has a tough time accepting our different way of life.

By the time Dick, the boys and I had all met back up again in Inyokern, California, Dick had a job lined up at China Lake, where he had worked previously for 17 years before we moved to Alaska, and would be starting work on Monday morning.

The boys and I went directly to the high school in Ridgecrest to get them enrolled so they could start right away as school was already in session. This was near the middle of September. We moved into my mother's house with the boys for the time being until we decided just what we were going to do.

Our oldest son, Robert, found a job at Padgett's Chevron station almost immediately and wanted to buy a motorcycle for his transportation. So Dick and I set up a payment plan for him and Robert was very happy to have his very first set of motorized wheels. He worked evenings and weekends and was so proud of his motorcycle. We were very proud of how well he handled his first large purchase and he never missed or was late with a payment.

Jeff, our youngest son, went right back into the local orchestra and picked up on his music performances like there was never a break.

Lucky for both boys that they knew many people from growing up in this area so that settling back in was not a problem. I was worried that the upset from another move might be too much but they handled it very well.

Then we had a surprise phone call after being back in California only a couple of weeks. The FAA (Federal Aviation Administration) wanted Dick to come to work for them in Barrow, Alaska. That was the one place that we did not want to live. We needed to have trees, mountains and water plus lots of greenery. It was so hard for Dick to turn that job down but he did. Then we had another call a few days later with an offer of an FAA position in Fairbanks which Dick accepted. He did ask that the pickup date for him be moved to December 1st. This would allow at least one month for the China Lake boss to find a replacement for Dick. We could also get more prepared for what we needed to do.

All of this called for a round table discussion with both boys to find out what they wanted to do at this time. The decision was made for the boys to finish out the school year in Ridgecrest, California. This was Robert's senior year of high school and he was signed up to go into the Navy just a short time after graduation. I would stay with the boys at my mother's house until school ended in June at which time Jeff and I would join Dick in Alaska.

We had most of the family together for the Thanksgiving holiday including Dick's mother and aunt from Santa Barbara, Dick's cousins from the San Fernando Valley and Bob W. and his mother. This was a fun celebration for us as we knew that our final move to Alaska was near and who knows when we will all be together again for a holiday season. As it turned out we managed to all get together again over Christmas 1981 back in Inyokern when we flew down for a two week holiday in California.

Chapter 10

PLANS CHANGE QUICKLY

Dick and I got busy figuring out just what he needed to take north with him. We sold the VW bus and bought a new Chevy pickup truck with a camper shell. Dick proceeded to put a block heater and battery heater blankets on the truck and change all lubricants to synthetics. This drew a lot of attention in the California desert when people would ask why we had a plug hanging out of the front grill! The next project was to find him a complete outfit of good winter outer wear. Dick would leave on December first with our dear friend Bob Weinhardt and drive to Fairbanks. We would not hear from him until he reached his destination. The boys and I stayed at Weinhardt's house to take care of his dog and house sit while he made this trip with Dick.

Dick and Bob had a great trip north even in the sub zero temperatures and long dark days. They were learning a lot about how vehicle seats stayed hard like cement until the interior of the truck warmed up in the mornings. Also how important it is to have arctic extension cords, after the regular cord Dick was using popped into many pieces when he tried to wrap it up after unplugging the block heater. They both laughed about these things and even how the tires seemed square when first starting out each day until the rubber warmed up on the roadway. Growing up in California we never had experience with REALLY COLD weather so it all seemed fun. Upon arrival in Fairbanks Dick and Bob found a motel room and started looking for a small economy apartment for Dick to live in. They were quite lucky to immediately find a small, clean, furnished, two bedrooms, apartment within two miles from the Fairbanks International Airport Tower where Dick would be working. The building was really off the road and had a huge gravel pit pond just a hundred feet from the door. This was a fairly quiet place to live and on the outskirts of town. Anyway, the guys moved into it and spent a couple of days driving around the area looking over Fairbanks in the winter time.

When Bob W. returned to California, the boys and I moved back to my mother's house and in a few days the boys asked for a family discussion. They seemed to be unhappy about our family being split up and thought we should all be together. In other words, they wanted to move back to Alaska NOW to be with dad too. This would have been more convenient to know a couple of weeks ago because we could have driven up with Dick. So we thought we would surprise Dick and just show up in time for Christmas. Thanks for VISA cards we were able to purchase three airline tickets and luggage to hold our things for our surprise flight. Our flight was to arrive in Fairbanks at midnight on December 23rd. I had already purchased some nice 35mm cameras for the boys as their Christmas gift and had them wrapped and hidden away. We bought some good winter clothing, filled our suitcases, stored Robert's new motorcycle at Bob W's house and checked the boys out of school. They had just taken all the exams and completed the first semester of the school year.

After thinking about the surprise for Dick we decided to call and let him know we would be there so he could shop for groceries for a nice holiday meal. I did not know if the stores would be open or even have the foods we wanted for Christmas that close to the holiday. At this time you must remember that fresh foods and such were commonly sold out early in Fairbanks. Thankfully Dick managed to get a turkey and all the trimmings for me to fix for our holiday together. He even had purchased bedding for the bed in the boy's room.

By now Robert had a serious girlfriend, Tina, the boss's daughter at the Chevron station where he worked. This was very hard for them to be separating and when we left Tina presented us with a lovely wooden pump planter box filled with a red Christmas candle, green spruce boughs and white spider mums flowers.

This was to be our Christmas tree at the new apartment since we would be arriving too late to do anything else about a tree. Well, I babied that lovely planter all the way north carrying it between my feet on the airline, with a long layover in Seattle where I carried it around but when we reached Fairbanks you will never guess what happened.

When we landed at Fairbanks International Airport it was announced that the outside temperature was 38 below zero with light snow falling. Boy, we were sure glad to see that Dick had gone out and purchased big military style parkas for the boys and me. He said to put them on before we go out to the truck. Dick, like everyone else left the truck idling with the heater going, so it would be warm to get into. It was so hard to even comprehend what minus 38 degrees was but as I stepped out the door into the cold the white spider mums in my lovely planter instantly turned dark brown and fell over like they had been shot. The boys, Dick and I were laughing so hard at this we could hardly cross the parking lot. At least the greenery and candle was looking good for our tiny Christmas tree! Then the boys discovered how much fun it was to run and slide on their feet across the parking lot and proceeded to play for a few minutes as Dick and I loaded the truck with our luggage. We were one happy family again! The deep cold wasn't as bad as expected.

By the time we all went to bed it was past 2am because we had a lot of catching up to do and we were exhausted. Christmas eve day was half over when we woke up. The boys went out to explore the neighborhood and walk to the University Mall about one mile away. I worked at baking and getting preparations done for our wonderful holiday feast. On Christmas morning the boys were surprised to find they each had a gift to open because we had agreed that our flight north was our gift for each other. They both had fun learning to use their new cameras and wanted more attachments which would come later at their birthdays. This was one of our finest Christmases as we each knew how precious it was just to be together again. I was very proud of our sons and what they gave up to move to Alaska at the ages of 15 and 17. At the time we thought how lucky we all are to have these experiences and still feel that way today.

After the holidays we went shopping for heavy snow pants, full face knitted hats and some trim to make my parka look more girlish. At the mall we found a sale and purchased ice skates for the boys as they had out grown their old ones. Then we all got out on that frozen pond in back of the apartment building and using snow shovels we plowed out a large ice rink and a track to race around and play on. It was great fun to walk out there and skate for awhile before returning to the apartment for hot chocolate and cookies. The four of us went ice skating quite often too. Then we had many nights we just went outdoors to watch the northern lights which are so awesome. To see the soft colors of green, yellow and pink dancing across the sky in so many different ways is hard to describe and we never get tired of watching the lights.

Robert and Jeff were enrolled in West Valley High School and settled in to their routine quite easily following the Christmas/New Years holiday season. They met a couple of other Johnson boys just down the road from us who were the same ages and became fast friends. It turned out that this Johnson family also owned a cabin on the Salcha River about three miles below us.

Here we are into January 1980 and our very first family winter in Fairbanks, Alaska. Every weekend we took a drive out a different road to just explore the area and see what it had to offer. We went to the dog sledding races, the local roller skating rink in North Pole several times, to all the winter carnival activities we could find and we even helped put up the famous tripod on the Tanana River in Nenana. It was so much fun to just get out and drive to any place for fun. February was a great month with so many activities going on around the small communities in the area. We only wished we could get out to our cabin. We needed snow machines to get up the frozen river and those would not come until the next year.

Dick and I would go for a walk each evening around what we called the block (a couple of miles) and always seemed amazed to see the beautiful northern lights. It was so interesting to learn that one can be quite comfortable even down to forty below zero when walking in the dark. That was the hardest part of all, getting use to it being dark most of the time. I think we made it easier by just staying busy and getting outdoors everyday for some activity. The boys were breaking ice skates many times due to the extreme cold so we limited their skating to 25 below zero or warmer. Jeff eventually took up cross country skiing and was often the only out there on the university ski trails when it was 30 below zero.

We were not able to get out to our cabin as we didn't have snow machines at the time. When the boys and I flew north commercially we had left our airplane in Inyokern, California. Without an airplane or snow machine we were stuck in town. We did not know enough about EXTREME cold weather flying yet so maybe this was a good break for us to learn more from other Alaskans. We sure did not want to get stuck in the bush causing Dick to lose his new job already. So we bided our time until the weather was nearer zero degrees for flying our plane that first year, plus we still had to bring the plane back north from the California desert.

One weekend in February, our new friend Don Hulshizer asked if Dick and the boys would like to travel up the river on snow machines and sleds. Don had two snow machines and sleds so they all loaded up and had a wonderful time for a couple of days. The boys were allowed to run the two snow machines all over the river by themselves while Don and Dick were at Hulshizer's cabin. The boys got stuck a few times but learned something new each time and seemed to take care of themselves pretty good. Of course, they all stopped in to check on our cabin and came home with some nice photos of all of them in the deep snow. I was actually jealous of missing out on this fun too. This weekend showed Dick how very important it was for us to get our very own snow machine for the next winter. We figured we could get by for now with one machine and a sled that would hold one passenger and a rider standing on the back. It was so much fun just going around and looking at all the machines that were available, gathering the information and then sitting home discussing and dreaming about the machines. Next winter we will have our own snow machine!

Chapter 11

YOU LEFT THE AIRPLANE SO GO GET IT!

By March of 1980 Dick and I were both missing our airplane. Since he was new on the job and would not have vacation time for a while he looked over at me and said, "You left the airplane in Inyokern so go get it!" I was flabbergasted and said, "But we still have a lot of snow out there!" To which he replied, "So by the time you get back up here it will be gone." Then we talked to the boys to see what they thought about Mom being gone for a couple of weeks. Everyone seemed to be quite happy with the thought of having our plane home with us. I was the only one who seemed to have some major concerns.

I know that I had already flown the airplane south from Fairbanks to Inyokern (3600 miles) just last September by myself with only my youngest son, 15 years old, along for the ride. The weather at that time was really mild and nice so we camped under the wings. Now I would be totally alone and flying over some desolate wilderness areas that still had a lot of snow. I can do this but I still had some doubts. Dick kept assuring me that if he did not believe in me he would never send me out to do the job. He said I was just as good a pilot as he was but I am not convinced!

Anyway, I soon had my airline tickets and had arrived at my mother's house for a couple of days to visit. My poor mother was having a fit about the idea of her little girl flying that distance all by herself but then she had the same fit when I flew in there last September! So when it came time for me to depart I left my mother, who was crying as she watched my takeoff, and I headed north to Alaska. By this time I was feeling pretty good about this flight and was singing at the top of my lungs NORTH TO ALASKA, GO

NORTH THE RUSH IS ON! I had made up my mind that this was only a bunch of small cross country trips from one point to another instead of looking at the overall picture. This made it easy.

I should have never drunk so much coffee with my mother this morning! There has been a bit of turbulence over the past hour flying along the east side of the Sierras close to the mountains. Now the coffee is telling me it all wants out! Drats! There is not an airport in my path for quite a while. Times like these it is nice being a man because any bottle will do for them to relieve themselves. Well, I soon spotted a nice cleared field that looked smooth so I landed and taxied over behind what looked like a barn. After taking care of my business I got back into my plane and as I was taxiing out for take off suddenly a woman appears out of a doorway in another building with a load of laundry. Since I didn't know what to do I just waved as I lifted off into the sky and she waved back at me. Then I laughed for quite a while as I thought about her reaction to a stranger landing in their plowed field, just to take a leak.

My first stop for the night was Alturas, California which sits at about 4000 feet. When I taxied in a man came out to help me park the plane as he remembered our plane from its many stops there. When he saw I was alone he told me to take the keys to his old pickup truck and go to town for dinner. When I came back I had a few items for my morning meal too. The FBO (fixed base operator) of the airport asked my plans for the night and I said that I was going to camp under my wing. At this he laughed and said, "Oh no, you are not! There is a storm coming in and we expect snow tonight. So here is the sofa in our lounge where you can sleep. Just be sure and lock the door when I leave and have the coffee ready by 8am. If the phone rings just answer it and take any messages for me. Does that sound OK to you?" Of course I was elated because it would be warm, soft and dry inside. I did not mind answering the phone. I telephoned Dick that night to let him know where I was and about the storm coming in. We are both hoping that I can move on in the morning.

Well, my stay in Alturas lasted for three days as I waited out a bigger snow storm than was expected. I drove into town once each day for a hot meal and spent each evening alone in the FBO office. I had coffee ready each morning and enjoyed talking with the many people who came by the airport. When I tried to pay the man he refused my money but wished me loads of luck on my journey north and wished he was doing such a trip too. After that we always stopped there to get fuel and visit the FBO when flying by the area. He was such a kind and thoughtful man.

Finally, on day three after a three night layover I was able to take off and head north again. Now I was wondering just how many delays I might encounter due to the weather. Oh well, don't worry about it, just keep flying and taking one day at a time. Things went along quite well and I was enjoying all the beautiful countryside. When flying alone it seems you are always busy following your maps, checking instruments, checking the skies for other aircraft and always looking for an emergency landing place. The time really flies by so to speak. I would only stop for fuel and then for the night so I was making good progress. This was before everyone had GPS systems so the navigation was still a challenge.

The next FBO that was special was the Shell distributor in Prince George, British Columbia. We had already flown through there several times and he knew us by now. When he heard that I was camping he insisted that I stay in their lounge on the sofa for the night. Again I was reminded to lock the door at night and please have the coffee going in the morning. Wow, this is so easy and makes for some special times. I would read until I fell asleep and wake up refreshed before opening time. I used the restrooms to freshen up and make myself look a bit neater. The next thing you know I was on my way once again.

The farther north you go the less traffic you see and it becomes like just you and the world out there. I would always call Dick at night to report in where I was so he could keep track. I made overnight stops in Watson Lake and Whitehorse in Yukon Territory and then a clearance stop for US Customs in Northway, Alaska. Wow, I am getting close to home now and excited to see the family again. When I was on my approach to Fairbanks International I started to get a bit nervous because I knew that Dick would be in the tower and everyone would be watching me land. It has always seemed that when one has a crowd you do your best screw ups and I really wanted to return in style with a perfect landing. This is sometimes hard to accomplish after several hours sitting but so far I have done great. Boy, what a relief to make a good landing and taxi right into transit tie down. Before I had turned the engine off Dick was out there to greet me!

As soon as I was back at the apartment I called my mother to let her know I had arrived in one piece and to tell her about the wonderful trip. Now she is even talking of maybe visiting us here one day!

We are now into May, the last month of the school year, and both boys seem to have done very well. In fact they were awarded for having perfect attendance for the whole school year, along with 10 other students. That seemed like a pretty small group to me but the reward was great. The High School Principal took these 12 students on a river rafting trip on the Nenana River near Denali National Park. The principal furnished all the food, soft drinks and complete trip in a school van which took them away on a school day for the whole day. To say the least, our sons were very happy indeed and had a great time. Many of their school friends were very jealous though.

The next event was for Robert to go on a senior trip out to the Chena Hot Springs Resort which was school sanctioned. Robert had a wonderful time and what a way to end your senior year. His high school graduation was really nice and we went out to a lovely dinner at the Switzerland before the ceremony as a family. We were so proud to see our first child graduate and become a man. Of course, this did not happen overnight as he was a man in training for several years. The sad part was now he was ready to leave for boot camp at the US Navy base in San Diego, California to begin his navy career. This summer was to be a great change in our family.

The FAA (Federal Aviation Administration) had notified Dick that he was to be sent down to Oklahoma City to attend a three month training course at the FAA Academy there. His school was to start about the middle of June. Jeff, our youngest son, and I would travel with Dick and stay in Oklahoma City for the long hot summer. We all flew as a family of four for the last time in our little Cessna 170 to California where we dropped off Robert for his Navy career. That was a tough goodbye because we couldn't even give Robert an address or telephone for us, except the FAA Academy for emergency only. Robert had absolutely no way to write or talk with us for more than three months. I think it was harder on me as Mom because one never expects to have a child leave home without any contact immediately following high school graduation. Thank heaven he seemed to be a pretty strong person and survived all this well. Of course, it helped him having a wonderful girlfriend not that far away from San Diego. I think the biggest hurt during this period was not having the money to travel to San Diego to see our son graduate boot camp training. We were very thankful that the Padgett family, which were to be Robert's future in-laws, and both our mothers were there. They gave us many photos of the occasion but I wanted to give Robert hugs personally. Robert even spent the 1980 holidays at Tina's family home in Ridgecrest that year where he proposed to Tina on Thanksgiving weekend. We are so proud of them both. It made me cry after Robert called to know he was moving on in life and we were not around to share in the excitement.

Our summer of 1980 in Oklahoma City has some very interesting points. The FAA put us up in a nice apartment complex with tennis courts and swimming pool. Jeff and I tried to get to know many other FAA families there but most had only small children. So I would get Jeff to go play tennis with me or we would swim. That was until it got so hot that Jeff blistered his feet right through his tennis shoes on the tennis courts. The swimming pool water was warmer than bath water so it was just cooler to stay in the air conditioned apartment. One of the FAA wives was doing acrylic painting on canvas so she was giving Jeff some lessons in painting that he seemed to enjoy. Thankfully we took along Jeff's guitar and he played a lot that summer. On the weekends we would take a city bus to the Crossroads Mall and just hang out for a few hours. Sometimes we would go to the movies or out to dinner.

That summer also brought a terrible sadness to us through the death of my mother's husband who had given her the best 18 years of her life. We received the message through the FAA since we were still in Oklahoma City and I took the next flight out for California. It was hard helping my mother cope with this loss and we were so thankful she was still working. Since Robert was still in basic training we chose not to interrupt his training as it would have made a big difference in his life at the time. So my mother and I along with my brothers and Les's three children held a simple graveside service right at Ridgecrest Cemetery. I was with Mom for about two weeks to help her get all of the legal affairs done and to take care of Les's things so life could go on as best as possible. Then I returned to Oklahoma City.

The next thing you know Dick, Jeff and I were all back in Fairbanks and the school year had started. Jeff was sort of lost without his brother as they had been the best pals forever. We soon found Jeff getting involved in his music playing the guitar more each day in his bedroom. I was worried that he needed friends. We would talk about Robert a lot. Jeff was getting good grades in school and seemed to be very well liked there. The banjo, violin and mandolin sat in Jeff's closet more now. Jeff even performed in a couple of competitions in town for a country-western recording contract. His performances were really great and he sang songs he wrote but it was hard to compete against the beautiful popular girls of the town. It was a good experience and we were proud of the performance he gave. Jeff did not get any recording contract but he continued to write songs which we liked very much.

During this time, while we were away from home, we had left our boat on the trailer stored in the Davis family yard just down river from the highway bridge across the Salcha River. These people had become good friends very quickly when we were moving up the river. We would park our truck and trailer in their yard where it was more protected than sitting in a deserted parking lot, since we were on the river for weeks at a time. Dick, Jeff and I would spend every weekend of the school year out on the river at the cabin and continued to work on the log walls of the addition. High school years are just too active for us to stay full time on the river and we only had a couple years left of school so we pushed our weekends to be as long as possible at our log cabin.

One weekend we had pulled into a service station for fuel and it was snowing. The vehicle next to us asked if we knew something he didn't because we were filling a boat and it was snowing out. We laughed and said no we just wanted to get in another weekend at our cabin.

The three of us really missed having Robert around working on our projects with us but that is just part of life. Our children grow up and have a life of their own, as it should be, but we miss them very much. We are just so grateful to have had such a close knit family during their growing up years.

As you can see we are having a hard time getting to stay out on the river but one must make a living and since Dick is in training he must attend schools all over the place. Dick really crammed a lot of education into a short period of time, the first two years with FAA, and was even able to take by-pass tests for several of his courses because he had been an electronics technician for many years prior to joining the FAA. During this time he went back and forth to Oklahoma City many times but Jeff and I only joined him that one time.

After both boys were gone from home Dick and I went to Sacramento, California for a 3-4 week FAA course and had some fun, when he wasn't in school, visiting many historical places there. Another time I joined him for a six week course in Anchorage where we had an efficiency apartment. We took our boat down to Anchorage and managed to spend a few weekends with our son, Jeff, who was living in Seldovia at the time. I really had time to run around and learn about all the shopping centers in Anchorage which has helped so much on our many returns to that huge city.

We try to do our best to raise our children to be healthy, independent and self supporting adults as well as to care about their friends and neighbors and help others in need. One never knows just how much of this sinks into their beings until later in life when they are grown. We are very fortunate that both our sons did well with the foundation they had as children. I guess when you feed children well, nurture them and give them a basic set of morals that will last them a lifetime; it will turn out well in the end. In this respect we have been very lucky indeed as both our sons are wonderful adults. Nobody is perfect and we did have our share of heartaches along the way but we can honestly say that today we are very proud of our family and what they stand for.

Chapter 12

SNOW MACHINE ADVENTURES

One cannot really enjoy Alaska winters without some snow machine adventures now and then. After spending the summer of 1980 dreaming of the snow season and studying all the information we had on machines we finally decided to go with a small Yamaha Bravo and a fold-a-sled. These were both fairly cheap and within our budget and would give us something to learn on. So sometime in October we purchased the machine and sled. Then we spent a weekend taking our little boat trailer apart and making it a flatbed so we could use it for double duty as a boat trailer or snow machine trailer. This was not hard to make as we removed all the boat rollers and slide rails then used 2x4 lumber and ¾ inch plywood for a flat bed. It came out pretty nice and we are still using the same trailer today.

Our first trip up the river to our cabin with our own snow machine and sled was so much fun. First of all we made sure we would have enough fuel by carrying two five gallon cans of gas. Then just in case we should run into problems we carried sleeping bags, small duffel of survival gear and an ice chest with hot water bottle to carry our food in so it would not freeze. It looked like we were on an expedition but we were prepared to take care of ourselves. Dick was going to drive the machine, Jeff would ride on the back of the sled and I would be inside the sled perched on the gas cans and sleeping bags. We would all be wearing goggles to protect our eyes because we did not learn until later that using helmets is really very important and much warmer too.

I think we traveled about 30 mph when on the frozen river but when in the woods on the bumpier winter trail we did 15-20 mph.

It was so gorgeous winding through the trees that were all flocked with glistening snow. I was amazed that one could see so easily even though it was dark because the stars, moon and northern lights keep things looking clear. You can walk around without a flashlight most of the time too. It was fun to watch for the various animal tracks and often we would see moose, ptarmigan and other small animals. Dick who was behind the windshield made many stops just to check on us passengers to be sure we were not getting frostbite on our faces. We actually looked like very interesting creatures in our bulky snow suits and faces covered with knit caps and our goggles on. While in motion we kept our parka hoods up to help our heads stay warmer.

By this time we had learned about "bunny boots" which are military issued heavy white rubber, insulated boots for the winter. These boots were made to keep your feet warm even when wet inside. We found the local Army Surplus Store and bought ourselves used bunny boots. Now we could travel in more comfort as our feet did get cold in our snow pac boots (with thick felt liners) after wearing them over many hours. One must remember to always take out the felt liners of your snow pacs when you are indoors so they will totally dry out. We use our snow pacs around home but when we are traveling for a long distance outdoors we wear bunny boots. Another great buy at the surplus store was some huge insulated mittens that you wear over your gloves. These mittens have a nice pile backing on the outside for wiping your nose off as it drips in the winter cold air. This freezes and can then be flicked off the pile quite easily leaving it clean for the next trip. The huge mittens come to your elbows with ropes to hold them around your neck when you want to slip them off for a few minutes but not lose them while working with just a thin gloved hand.

When we arrived at our cabin and opened the door it was colder inside than it was outside so we left the door open while we started a fire and unloaded the sled. There are several Aladdin lamps and regular kerosene lamps in the cabin so we lit them all to give us light and added heat. These turned into normal operating procedures for us over the years. The cabin was not insulated at this time and had no ceiling, only the roofing and three small windows. Since we had it packed full of our things it was much harder to heat because there is not much room for air circulation and everything inside is “chock a block cold” which must thaw before you start to feel heat. All of this takes time so you arrive cold and try to keep warm by moving around doing anything. We found that a good solid chocolate bar does wonders for helping one feel warmer. Another good nourishing item was frozen peanut butter chipped off in big chunks to suck on like candy. The first thing on the stove is a bucket of ice to thaw for our water. We always leave a couple of buckets of water covered with a towel and some firewood handy so you have the necessities upon arrival. We were all having a great time believe it or not!

Often on our rides out on the river Dick would ride the sled and let Jeff drive the snow machine. One particular day when we were headed down to the highway Jeff was driving and we had several places with open water on the river. The worst places were near clear ice without snow on top so the machine and sled could get into an out of control slide on the ice. This sometimes left you headed right towards open water! No one wants to go into open water when it is 20 below zero and colder so we all tend to avoid the ice under high power and slowly make our way around the bad spots. On this day Jeff was moving along about 30mph and didn’t realize that the sled was drifting right across a hole in the ice. I proceeded to jump off the sled and so did Dick to keep from going into the hole. Dick said, “There goes our son off into the sunset without a care!” That made us both start laughing so hard we could hardly stand up. Anyway, we proceeded to walk about a mile down the river waiting to hear Jeff returning for us. Jeff had no idea what had happened and could not hear us yelling for him over the sound of the engine. Then he drove about five miles before he stopped where we were to change drivers. Jeff got mad because he thought we had hidden in the bushes to just scare him. When Jeff yelled out our names several times and he did not get a reply he knew we had fallen in the river somewhere. Jeff was so scared that it didn’t take him long to turn the machine around and when we heard him coming the machine was really screaming at full throttle. Dick and I couldn't help laughing when he pulled up looking scared to death. We then asked him how long before he even looked back to check on his passengers and he told us. To say the least, Jeff did not think any of this was funny but it turned out to be a lesson well learned about travel in the bush. This mistake was never made again. We always keep a check on each other when traveling.

On another trip going up the river with Dick driving and Jeff and I on the sled we lost control on a long patch of clear ice and the machine was spinning right out over some deep water. Jeff jumped clear and stayed on the frozen ice pack while Dick and I went into the water. Luckily the hole was fairly small so the skis on the front of the snow machine hung up on the ice out front and the back of the sled also hung up on the opposite side of the hole putting the two pieces of equipment in a big V shape mostly under water. Dick and I were submerged to the chest. Now we were a bit concerned and needed to get our equipment out of the water in temperatures hovering around 25 below zero. Dick wanted me to get out and help Jeff by each of us pulling on the skis of the machine while Dick tried to raise the back of the machine up to the ice.

Every time I tried to get out of the water I would splash water up onto the ice and cause myself to slide right back down again. After several tries I was getting exhausted and just laid my arms with big mittens onto the ice for a rest. When I tried to get out again my mittens had frozen to the ice and I was able to use them to help pull myself up. Now that was a good lesson learned at the time. Do not fight the situation but freeze your mittens to the ice to use as leverage to pull yourself out of the hole. Most of all do not panic as that can kill you.

Anyway, now both Jeff and I are on top of the ice and Dick is worried that we may not be able to get the equipment back onto strong ice. We all three struggled for several minutes and we were not any closer to having the machine on top of the ice. Suddenly Jeff stopped to open his camera case and was going to take a picture when Dick yelled at him to throw the camera aside and help! Later

Dick wished we had a photo of that encounter.

I was getting so cold that I said we should start a fire on the gravel bar to warm up some. Dick proceeded to reach down into his pocket and hand me a soggy book of matches which made me furious. I asked him where the new waterproof wooden matches and cases were that both he and Jeff were given. Both of them answered, "Back in town." With this we all three cracked up in laughter at the stupid situation, which seemed to renew our strength and on the next pull we had the machine and sled out of the water. Dick quickly drained the fuel tank from the bottom to remove any water until it ran with gas, dried out the spark plugs, pulled the starter rope several times before we were back in business!

Now you probably think that is the end of that story but as we piled onto the machine and sled trying to get home so we could dry out and warm up we had another incident. Dick was trying to stay clear of the water in another place a few miles farther up river when he hit an ice chunk suddenly tipping the sled which threw me out into the shallow water on the gravel. Jeff riding on the back runners had more control and was able to stay upright. Now this was the last straw because I was so cold already, I was not able to warm up after a second dunking. Since we were only a couple of miles from home we kept moving. I assured Dick that I would be fine, just get me home ASAP!

By the way, we did learn another good lesson about soaked clothes on this trip. Just stand still and let the outside of your clothing freeze and you will remain warmer on the inside but do not go for another dip as that will not work twice in succession. Thankfully we always had extra clothes at the cabin and were able to dry off and put on dry clothes immediately. Jeff worked at starting the fire and before long we were three happy but tired characters!

This was the beginning of a tradition for us until Jeff was through with school for the summer. Every Friday afternoon when Jeff got home from school we would be sure to have all the stuff ready so we could leave for the river as soon as Dick came through the door after work. I made bean burritos ahead of time which we ate while driving the 44 miles out to the river parking lot and we carried warm drinks. The three of us crowded into the seat of the pickup truck and visited while eating dinner on the drive. Then we quickly loaded the boat or sled (depending on the time of year) and headed out up the river or trail to our place for the weekend. We could hardly wait to get there but a lot of the fun was in the journey.

Sometimes when running on the river you can run into trouble with holes in the ice, thin ice or just plain open leads of water with clear ice where the snow has blown off leaving very slick trail conditions. We were no different than anyone else out doing the same things and ran into our share of trouble at times. It may seem a bit scary to realize that we were traveling about 60 miles round trip each weekend on only one snow machine but there was always many other people traveling back and forth as well even if we hardly ever saw them.

By the next winter we had a second identical snow machine and that made the trip much easier. The new machine was mine and I was to drive it all the way to the cabin for the first time. I was so happy having my own brand new machine and really enjoyed the trip until we came to our place on the river and there was a 3-4 foot wide strip of open water right along our river bank where our ramp went up into the yard. Now Dick had been studying snow machines and their uses and said that you just give it some throttle and run right across the lead of water and up the bank into the yard. Then Dick, with Jeff riding the sled, took off and ran right across the water and up the bank. They both yelled back to me to just hit it fast so I did just what they said but when I came up the bank I was totally airborne and headed for a big tree. They are both yelling BRAKES but I was moving so fast that the next thing I knew my machine and I had climbed about four feet up a large spruce tree. I had one ski on each side of the tree with my machine now sitting on the backend. The tree broke my front bumper and bent the tub some. When I came down from my flight on my left knee against the rear bumper it broke the bumper as well. Both Jeff and Dick came running over to see if I was OK. Dick saw me crying and wanted to know where I was hurt and all I could say was, "Oh, my pretty new machine is damaged!" My knee was hurting some but I staggered up the steps into the cabin and did not realize until later that night how bad I was hurting. No, I did not see a doctor and just limped around for a few weeks until I could resume normal duties. I was so upset about my machine but before long Dick had it all fixed up and looking just fine. The machine was a little scratched which Dick calls giving it character but ran like new again. In fact I drove that machine for over ten thousand miles before we bought new machines again.

Since we are onto snow machine stories I have to relate a couple of dumb and funny things Dick and our sons have done. Like taking snow machines out onto a frozen lake and spinning them around in circles at high speed, occasionally leaving a rider flying off from the centrifugal forces. I will never understand how they always came home laughing and not hurt one bit. Another thing they would play at was hauling each other on the back of a sled across really rough country trying to see who could stay on the sled the longest. I think all three of them were dumped off head first into a snow bank over a period of time. There was always some sort of competition going on between the three of them which was a riot to watch. Age doesn't seem to matter at all as boys will be boys forever in life!

One winter when Dick and I were alone, after both boys had grown up and left home, we were headed up the winter trail on our double wide snow machine (1979 Skidoo Bombardier). This machine looked like a bright yellow little tank with bucket seats side by side, a roll bar for protection and you climbed into it over the side. We called this machine SHERM, after the Sherman Tanks of WWII. Sometimes the creek crossings at Redmond Creek and McCoy Creek were very unstable with bad ice which made it a challenge to cross the creeks but we had to get home.

We had stopped to really check out the crossing at Redmond before driving out onto the ice. Often we would have to build a ramp of snow and branches to get down the bank and back up the bank on the other side. Dick even walked across tamping the ice with a large broom handle we carried for a walking stick and came back declaring the crossing safe. I was afraid of the ice so Dick drove the snow machine across first and I watched the ice sway down badly underneath him, telling me the ice was thin. So that is when I said I was not walking across that ice! Dick walked back over to me told me to walk right where he had gone. So I figured if he walked it twice, then drove a big heavy machine across I should be able to just walk easily and follow in his tracks. As I neared the far bank suddenly the ice cracked and broke out leaving me floundering around in the water and I could not touch bottom. Dick ran over to grab my hand and pull me up the bank and proceeded to pull my glove off when I was almost up to the top of the bank which dropped me right back into the water. Dick tried several things to get me out but with wet clothes and all it was just too much for him. Finally, he threw a rope to me and said to tie it around under my arms so he could get more leverage and this time I popped right out of the water and up the bank. I was shivering so hard I thought my teeth would crack! Dick helped me into the snow machine and we took off for the nearest cabin that we knew had firewood so I could strip and get warm and dry. That was one long ride when you are freezing cold! We even returned some firewood to the cabin where we stopped because we knew someone else might need it badly someday.

After we were living full time on the river Dick commuted every day to work mostly by airplane, which in the winter time can be a real challenge at best. Of course, we did have a cut off temperature for flying our Cessna 170 that was 30 below zero. When it was that cold and colder Dick would drive a snow machine to the highway approximately 30 miles and then take our truck into town 44 miles to the airport where he worked. This was a two hour commute one way. Sometimes when I had shopping to do I would run into town with him and this one particular day we were traveling together on snow machines. After having some warm weather we had a lot of overflow water on the river ice which was turned into slush ice overnight. This is very hard to see when it is crusted over in the wee dark hours of early morning.

As I came around a corner I watched Dick's headlight go out about one quarter mile ahead of me so I stopped and tried to see what had happened. Dick yelled back to me to stop right there and wait. He was stuck in some deep overflow and had filled the sled with slush ice. At the spot where he sat at the time he had a few feet of good solid ice so he turned the machine around by hand and pulled it back to give him the greatest distance for a strong start. Then he hollered to me to turn on my headlight so he knew where to aim his machine. I was to be ready at the edge of the good ice to grab his ski and pull to help him get back onto safe ice. As it turned out he was almost stopped when he reached the good ice but not quite on top of the good ice and my pulling on the ski saved another dunking in the deep slush. This process seemed to work just fine and soon he was standing beside me telling me that the overflow went bank to bank across the river and we could not go that way.

Dick was wet, cold and in a hurry now so he would not be late to work. We quickly back tracked to our cabin where he put on dry clothes and we took the winter trail down to the highway. You probably wonder why we did not take the trail in the beginning but most of us run on the river when we can because it is smoother and much faster. The trail can be very bumpy and slow. As it turned out Dick was fine getting to work as we always leave enough time for whatever delays come up.

By winter of 1984 I became confident enough to make trips into town on my own using a snow machine to get to the highway about 30 miles, then our truck to go into town (44 miles) shopping. I would leave the cabin about 7am and arrive in town by 9am. By the time I completed shopping and went to lunch with friends it was late in the afternoon. Then I headed back to the Salcha River Lodge where I would repack and load all my supplies on the sled and head home, arriving home between 7-9pm. After getting my fire started, unloading the sled and putting the fresh goods away I was really tired. Each trip was quite a workout but a lot of fun too. I have always enjoyed those lovely night runs when the moon is out and the world looks like a fairy winter wonderland.

Over the years of snow machine travel we have experienced many hazards but have usually had the time to fix, repair or go around a trail problem. The most dangerous is crossing the not quite frozen creeks and running into holes in the river ice. Several years ago some of our neighbors got together and built a bridge across the two biggest creeks, Redmond and McCoy, but the flood waters often wash the bridges away. They have been rebuilt many times over the years. These bridges are sometimes just a couple of long trees spanning the creek with cross boards nailed on a few inches apart. The bridge is a flat deck with no side rails and only inches wider than our snow machine and sled. When the snows are very deep these bridge crossings can be tricky because soon the tracks ice over making the sled slide around. So far no one has ever gone over the side that we know of. The reason the bridges were built in the first place was because the water did not freeze solid enough to drive on and often that trail is the only way you can get to the highway. It is nice to have travel options when living so far from the road.

Sometimes we have early wet heavy snows in the fall that break small trees and branches blocking the winter trail. There are even many beaver cut trees that fall and block the way too. Beaver must always be chewing on trees to keep their teeth in good condition. We always carry a chain saw during these times to make it easier to cut and clear the trail. One year it took us two weekends with several people working together to cut the trail open. That is a lot of work, more than you can imagine. We always laugh when people ask us if we exercise often and we tell them to just follow us around for a while and see how much exercise we get just from living each day!

Chapter 13
EMPTY NEST

By the summer of 1981 we had finished the outside of our addition to the cabin and just in time. In June we had our son's friend from California coming up to spend the summer with us as a high school graduation gift. John would actually be here in time to help do the roofing of the new room. Then Dick's mother was coming for a visit for a couple of weeks too. This was to be quite a social summer for us. Dick and I rushed to get the bedrooms in order before Mom arrived. We had made a big bed for us at one end of the room with a wood rod holding lined curtains to divide the room in half. At the other end was the boys bunk beds and we used a blanket off the end of the bunks to make a small divide for a roll away bed for Mom to use. I had put down small throw rugs and tried to decorate a bit with pictures to make it feel more like home.

We had a great time with John as he was like another son to us so after the boys had been working their little hearts out for us we thought it would be good for them to have some new experience. The boys were to get train tickets to go from Fairbanks to Denali Park where they would spend a week in a walk in camp ground and explore in the National Park by bus. The boys took our boat to the highway where they loaded it onto the trailer and parked it over at Davis's. Then they drove the truck into town where they had to purchase all the food and snacks they needed for their excursion. We would not see them or hear from them until their return. While in town they also did a few tourist things together so John would have some vacation memories to take home.

At times during the days on the river Jeff would tell John that he could hear a fish calling and they would go to the river bank and fish for a short time with Jeff catching fish each time. John thought this was so funny. One day when Dick and I had taken Mom to town for some tourist trip we left the boys at the cabin. When we returned the boys had the cabin all cleaned up with a bottle of our homemade cranberry wine on the table and a plate of Ritz crackers and a grayling spread (our local fish from the river) for a pre-dinner snack for all of us. There was even a small bouquet of wildflowers in a glass on the table. That was so nice and thoughtful of the boys.

I think that both John and Mom had a summer to remember. The biggest complaint from both of them was they did not like putting on mosquito repellant, finding a new hatred for mosquitoes. Dick and I wore repellant like a deodorant every day.

Mom liked having her coffee with cream and sugar and the mosquitoes loved the muddy looking warm drink as well. Mom was always picking the dead mosquitoes off the top of her coffee which gave all of us a laugh! So to make her feel normal around us, on our next trip south to visit her in California, our son had taken a small bottle with a couple of dead mosquitoes to put in her coffee while we were there. To say the least this brought hails of laughter all around.

We had been informed that our son, Robert and Tina would be getting married in August 1981 in Ridgecrest, California so we had to make plans for a trip south. This would cut John's summer trip short but we were not going to miss this wedding. We flew our Cessna 170 to Ridgecrest. I can verify that August is not the time to get married in the desert as the temperatures were hovering around 116 degrees, breaking records, during the days of the wedding. Both of our families had been friends for many years so we were having a great time together. I have never been to such a lovely formal wedding with a reception following in the church social hall, where the air conditioner quit working! Our youngest son was best man for his brother and we were so proud to watch the two of them all dressed up and behaving like real men. The groom was in his dress Navy uniform and the bride was exquisite in a lovely floor length flowing Victorian gown and veil. It was one of those bitter sweet moments knowing we would never have little boys again. The partying went on for a while and then the men decided to help pack a rented trailer with all of Tina's things and their wedding gifts for the newlyweds drive to Washington before starting on their honeymoon to Alaska. It was funny to watch all the men in tuxedos packing the trailer. I couldn't wait to get out of my dress and pantyhose and into cooler clothes.

By the time we arrived back at our cabin in Alaska the newlyweds had spent a week there in the peace and quiet. They had one interesting story to tell about coming around a corner in the river and having the boat engine quit leaving them free floating backwards towards a log jam. Thankfully they were close to a neighbor's cabin and he saw them in trouble. The neighbor, Dick Deweese helped them out immediately. Our poor new daughter-in-law was getting quite an adventure now. I think this was a bit of a shock to Tina as many of us seem to be a bit rough around the edges for her liking. She was such a sweet, quiet girl but it did not take long for her to learn how to joke around with the rest of us. We wished the kids the best of love and luck in their future and they headed home to Washington where Robert was stationed at Whidbey Island Naval Air Station. Tina had fun fixing up their apartment and making it into their home.

On Dick's airline trips through Seattle going to Oklahoma City for other FAA schools he would always stop to visit Robert and Tina. The first meal that Tina served her father-in-law she produced a plate with a big rubber hamburger as a joke for Dick because he always teased her about never wanting to eat anything but hamburgers. Dick still has the rubber burger and we laugh about it after all these years.

Before we knew it the final senior year of high school for Jeff had started. He was having fun taking a few shops and even doing some office practice. Since Jeff was really into flying he took the FAA ground school class during this year of school and found out how much there is to know before getting ones pilot license. Jeff had decided he wanted to go into the US Navy and went down with his dad to sign up for the early enlistment program just like Robert had done. So now we know that as soon as he graduates he will be leaving for basic training in San Diego, California. That will mean another few months without knowing how things are going in his life. It is times like this that I would love to have a telephone out at the river cabin but there is no services out there.

Dick, Jeff and I flew on commercial airline down to California for the Christmas holiday 1981 and met up with Robert and Tina, both of our mothers, Aunt Jessie and friends for a wonderful family holiday together. Tina, Robert's wife, is pregnant and looking so cute. They expect their baby in May 1982. We are so excited about becoming grandparents! We are finding it great fun to watch our grown sons mature.

We tried to make this last year of our family life fun and spent a lot of time running snow machines and having fun together. Then came May 1982 and Jeff's high school graduation exactly two years after Robert. The irony of both of our sons starting basic training on June 9th two years apart seemed odd. We laughed about children growing up and you break their plates to send them on their way to adult life. Well we did not break plates but flew them to another state and dropped them off! That is so sad really.

Dick and I moved out to the river full time at the end of May 1982 and gave up the apartment in town that was used on school days only. Every thing we owned was now on the river except for our highway vehicle and trailer. I was having fun as we had insulated the cabin and made board and batt lumber (barn style) for a ceiling in the cabin. These boards were made from trees that we fell in our yard and then cut into lumber using a chain saw sawmill. Dick and Jeff had made me a cute corner triangle cabinet for my china using only a chainsaw and the top front of the cabinet had a glass door. We made a couple of windows bigger to let in more light and put up second panes for more insulation at the windows for winter. I started sewing red checkered valances for the windows to match the curtains across the kitchen cupboards and was busy cutting brush trying to make a larger yard. It was feeling a bit closed in so I thought having more room and more sunshine would help. It seemed we were always busy with some building project or another and getting firewood cut, split and stacked for the winter. We like to have a big pile and stay ahead of the game just in case you have a time of illness or something to prevent one from cutting wood.

It did not take me long to get a bit depressed from the empty nest syndrome. Oh how I missed my boys and would write to them regularly. I knew that this was the way life should be and I should be happy that we had done as good a job of parenting as we knew how but I was feeling so empty. That is when I started doing a lot more volunteer services for others. I also got busy on many new knitting projects and other handcrafts. I went back to reading a lot of books, learning to can meats and other things.

Then it was berry picking time and that kept me busy for a few days before having to process them and make jams or whatever we wanted. That fall we were given half of a moose, our first wild meat in Alaska, for helping a neighbor to gut, skin and transport the moose right here on the river. I was so excited to see that meat hanging in our yard and waiting for me to process it. Well, let me tell you that one half of a moose is one heck of a lot of meat! I spent four days cutting roasts, steaks, stew meat, and hand grinding burger meat while canning in between. I have two huge pressure cooker canners and kept them both going on the stove about 14 hours a day. It takes about 4 hours to cold pack the meat and pressure can and set out to cool one load of jars (14 pints or 7 quarts). Take that times two canners and you can see how many jars I ended up with. We will have meat for the next two years! I also would fish and can grayling which we used in place of tuna for sandwiches, casseroles or dips. These things kept me busy but it was rewarding work. There is nothing like the satisfaction one feels from putting up their own food supplies.

Then in October we had a letter from Jeff saying he was going to be married on November 13th and hoped we could make it down to California for his wedding. Well, this was a real shock since we were not even aware that he had been seriously dating anyone. Thankfully it was a girl he had grown up around and we knew both her and her family quite well. We wondered if Jeff was just in a hurry to be like his older brother and tried to talk him into waiting until next summer but they said NO to us. Jeff was so young and immature but his mind was set on marriage. Now we were trying to shuffle work schedules and try to get things worked out for us to make a trip south at the last moment. Robert was to be his brother's best man so both our sons were in the wedding once again. Jeff and Tammy had chosen to marry down at Saline Valley Hot Springs which was very remote and isolated so most of our relatives were not able to attend the wedding. The wedding did turn out to be quite lovely and we had a fun weekend camping out with our old friends. The newlyweds were packing up soon and off to his new tour of duty back in Washington, DC, on the Presidential Honor Guard. They had great fun setting up housekeeping in an old apartment and made it look very nice. Tammy had a job real soon with the government and they made some good friends in Manasses, Virginia where they would go on weekends.

Christmas of 1982 was our first holiday season being totally alone since we always had someone living with us up to that point in our marriage. My younger brother was living with us and then we started our family. This was a hard holiday to get through and many of the Christmas carols over the radio made me cry. I finally got busy baking cookies and making trays of goodies to take to our friends and neighbors. Then I knitted several pairs of mittens with matching caps and took them to the homeless shelter in town which really made me feel better. At this time there were several families living about 15 miles up river from us and we all got together for dinners, cookie exchange, and just fun.

Since Dick worked with several younger men that had children at home, he volunteered to work the holiday so they could be with their families. I went ahead and planned to have our dinner ready when he came home that Christmas night. I was using the propane range cook top when I started cooking but the temperatures dropped lower than 40 below zero and the propane quit working. Now this was a new challenge for me but I had the wood heater going and thought I would just finish cooking over it. Since I did not have an oven I was using a Coleman camp oven on top of a barrel wood stove. The Coleman oven is about a 12 inch cube and can only take one pie at a time or another baked dish. I found a small ten pound turkey that would fit into the oven but had to put it in with the oven tipped over a bit so the pan with the turkey could go in the door crosswise. It took me all day to prepare our meal but it turned out just fine and we had a nice time that evening. It was so very quiet but we had each other, a warm cabin and lots of friends up the river. Oh how I missed our sons though. I guess every mom goes through this once in her life but it was not fun. I wondered if I should be doing something more with my life now but I still had a husband and a home that took up much of my time which I felt was very important too.

Then in January 1983 we had a phone call from my brother telling us that my mother had a stroke and was in need of some very special attention for rehabilitation. In fact the doctors were not sure she would ever walk again. I immediately went to town and caught an airline to California to see what I could do to help. My mother had a very serious aneurysm at the base of her brain and if that should break she would be dead. After talking with her doctors and the rehab personnel I decided that we could accomplish more with Mom keeping her at home and doing the rehab work several times a day with her. This new situation looked like I would be down in California with Mom for a long while so when I told Dick about the circumstances he said that he would put in for a temporary transfer back to China Lake so we could be together. Thankfully both his FAA boss and the China Lake people worked to help him with this problem. This made us both so sad because our hearts were still on the Salcha River and we were having one terrible time trying to stay put there.

In the meantime I worked with my mother daily giving her the care she needed and doing physical therapy several times a day with her. I promised her that she would walk again within a year and be back to almost normal. This was a real struggle at times because Mom would try to give up and I would not let her. Mom had to learn to talk, write, walk, feed and take care of herself all over again. With persistence we managed to have Mom attending her church services using only a walker by the end of that year. I was so thankful to have many friends to help cheer me when I would get down emotionally.

About three weeks after I told Dick that I was staying in California to help Mom, he called me to ask me to meet him in Seattle. Dick drove our pickup truck with a few personal items in the back of the truck down to Seattle and he used my return airline ticket to go back to Fairbanks to get our airplane and fly south. I drove the truck south to Inyokern, California. My brother stayed with Mom for those couple of days. Soon Dick joined us and we started a new phase of our life as caregiver to my mother. This can be one tough job and takes so much patience but we were thankful that we could make the time to care for Mom. Mom was a very special lady.

About one year later Dick and I were moving out of Mom's house to rent a small cabin back in Kennedy Meadows where we stayed after selling our home up there in the High Sierras. I would go to Mom's house almost daily to help her get adjusted to living alone once again. Mom needed a lot of reassurance that she could do this and after another year went by Dick called to get transferred back with the FAA in Fairbanks, Alaska. This all fell into place so nicely and right away, that Dick and I were on cloud nine knowing we could go home. That is when Mom decided she wanted to live close to us and chose to make the move to Alaska with us when we returned.

So much for us getting use to living alone! We packed up Mom's furniture and things had a moving company come and pick it up for delivery to Fairbanks. Mom's trailer home sold easily and we loaded up for our trip north after two years in California. We are now into February 1985 and just before leaving Inyokern my older brother and his youngest son decided to drive north with us. My brother had a van with all of his valuables and would follow us. We told him that if he had problems we would not be able to wait for him because Dick had a time line to report to work and we were not going to screw that job up.

While I was completing all the details for Mom's move to Alaska Dick left in our airplane to fly to Fairbanks where he would leave our plane and return to Seattle by airline. Mom and I drove our pickup truck north to Seattle where I had some new tires installed on the truck. We met up with my older brother and his son before picking up Dick at Sea-Tac airport to make the drive north from there. The trip up the Alaska Highway in the winter is really gorgeous and very desolate with few businesses open beyond the small towns. Dick and I started singing a song as we drove along using the tune from "I Never See Maggie Alone". The words we sang were "she brings her mother, brother and nephew along and I never see KayD alone". My Mom kept asking when the snow would end and Dick told her in May! Of course, Mom thought Dick was joking. Traveling with mom was fun because she was like a child seeing everything fresh for the first time with a lot of oohing and ahhing. Dick never tired of answering her questions along the way.

We were unable to find a winter coat and boots for Mom before leaving Seattle as the stores in the lower 48 states had put away winter gear and had spring clothing out already. So we waited until we reached Prince George, British Columbia and finally found a parka and snow pac boots for Mom. Mom's reaction was, "My God, I can't wear that stuff because the coat is too bulky and the boots are cumbersome!" When Dick told her she must wear these to survive poor Mom started wondering if she made a mistake moving north. It was really fun to watch the transformation of Mom to Alaska and it did not take her long to be happy about her move.

My brother and his son would meet up with us each evening at our motel stops and we would have dinner together and discuss the day's journey. All went well until we reached the Fort Nelson, British Columbia area where my brother had a vehicle break down and had to stay for repairs. He said he would catch up with us down the road and he did at Watson Lake, Yukon. It was a wonder because he had to drive very fast to make up the time but was knocking on our motel room door at 5am.

After reaching Fairbanks Mom was convinced the snow was around forever! My brother and his son decided to stay and work for a while so they rented a place and found jobs driving taxi cabs. We found a nice apartment on the ground floor for temporary housing for Mom until we could find a house to purchase. Mom was surprised to see the depth of snow in the yard but also glad to know there was some nice shopping centers in town. In fact, my brother and his son spent a lot of time in that apartment too.

In April 1985, our son Robert, Tina and their two children flew up bringing our youngest son, Jeff, home after he had some physical problem and trouble with his life. Jeff was now separated from his wife and new baby daughter. We had a fun filled Easter holiday with our two grandchildren and even took them all out to the cabin for a few days.

Soon our son, Jeff, had a job driving a taxi cab in Fairbanks and trying to decide what to do with the rest of his life. It was hard to watch the struggles going inside our son, Jeff, and knowing that we could not do anything to help except to be there when needed and give lots of hugs and love. This was a very difficult time

By June 1985 we were moving Mom into a nice house, three bedrooms and two baths, in a lovely new neighborhood after weeks of house searching. We wanted to purchase something a bit out of town but Mom wanted to be right along a highway where she could watch the traffic. This was a compromise but Mom was happy when her furniture arrived and we finally had her settled in her new home. Dick and I bought the house and made the payments thinking it was a good investment but we always called it Mom's house. The extra bedrooms were for Dick's mother and aunt should they ever need care as it would put the three ladies close for us to take care of. I spent a couple of weeks in town with Mom taking her out to the senior center several days a week, to a church on Sundays and shopping at the various small malls. This was to give Mom some good orientation to her new town and help her meet people her own age. Mom was very outgoing and easy to know so my job here was not difficult. I would do all the main housekeeping and yard work while Mom was responsible for cooking, laundry and taking care of herself. This worked out very well as Mom loved to do handcrafts and immediately started making hook rugs and doing crewel embroidery throw pillows. Soon she had visitors coming to her home which she loved. My brother and nephew John would drop in to visit Mom often too. Our son, Jeff stayed in one of the spare bedrooms until he could get his bills paid off and be able to get on his own.

At this time Dick and I started to spend more time on the river again splitting the week into four days on the river and three days in town at Mom's. During that summer Mom had me painting the outside of the house and the complete interior plus wall papering parts of the kitchen and main bathroom. Then we hauled rocks from a quarry and lined flower beds before hauling soil and plants to make the house look like a real home with color. Mom was a great supervisor and I did a good job at all the grunt work.

Everyone seemed to be happy and we lined up a couple of nice trips for Mom to take with a lady companion the same age and physical condition. The two women spent eight days in Hawaii having a wonderful time and learning so much about the Polynesian culture. Mom flew to Fort Yukon and other small places in the interior of Alaska. It was safe to say that my mother was having the time of her life as she had never traveled much before. We were so glad that Mom made friends so easily and soon had a life of her own going quite well. It was great to see Mom so happy and involved with living. Mom even had a new gentleman friend that loved to take her for rides and picnics so we got out of the house often.

CHAPTER 14

DEATH CHANGES EVERYTHING

One week during the summer of 1985 we took my mother with us in the boat to our cabin. She was not impressed at all and could not imagine anyone wanting to live so far away from everything. Now this was not the first time Mom had seen our place because she had made a trip to Alaska on the State Ferry System back in 1981 after trying to get over the death of her husband, Les in June of 1980. That trip was great as Mom had her very first airline ride to Seattle, the three day ferry trip up the inside passage with stops in several towns, then by train from Skagway over the mountains to Whitehorse, Yukon and tour bus into Fairbanks. We spent a few days in town taking Mom to several good tourist places, the museum and then a few days on the river with us. I was so glad that I was able to plan such a great overview of Alaska for her first trip and talk her into making the biggest trip of her life, at that time. Our boat trip on the Salcha River scared Mom and she hated the mosquitoes but remained a trooper all the same.

Now back to the time when Mom lived in Fairbanks during 1985-86, she came up the river only one time and never wanted to come back. Mom liked to be in town with all the amenities too much! Mom also had a man friend she met at the senior center who would take her to dinner, on picnics and drives now and then. So we each had our own little worlds and yet were able to share in many things together. I felt very lucky to have had the last 23 years with my mother as one of my best friends.

Our family fell into a nice routine and Dick and I were happy to be back on the river most days of the week. This was the summer of 1985 and we proceeded to do some remodeling in our cabin by first tearing out the old kitchen cupboards. Then we pounded in a driven point well for about 20 feet which was quite a job. The well point piece of pipe was about three feet long with holes along the sides to let water in. Someone on the river had a pipe well driver with about a 100 pound weight and a cross pipe at the top for a handle. This weighted pipe would fit right inside the 1 ½ inch galvanized pipe that we were using for a well. With Dick and I on each side of the pipe using one handle each we would raise and lower the weighted driver and pound the well point into the ground. Every five feet we would add another section of galvanized pipe. After about three hours we had a well with water and the pipe ended right at the top of the kitchen counter. Dick built new cupboards that ran the length of one wall in the main cabin room with a lovely countertop, double stainless steel sink and a cute red hand pitcher pump right at the sink. Then we ran a sewer line from the sink out to a newly dug 8x8 foot cesspool which was lined with logs. We covered the hole with logs and put about two feet of soil back on top. I was so excited to have a nice red pitcher pump with running water right at the double sink in the kitchen and even a drain from the sinks outdoors. Now this was getting to be easy living!

We put in a board and batt ceiling in the bedroom area with lumber we had made from our own trees using a chain saw mill. Then we installed a fringe area TV antenna with a booster and started to join in the modern world with four local stations from Fairbanks. Dick bought me a microwave oven and made a cabinet for that and the TV. I was feeling like a queen. We even installed carpeting on the cabin floor. Our little cabin was looking pretty good and we were beginning to have neighbors drop by now and then to visit. This made us feel like we were really part of the Salcha River community for sure.

The winter progressed and we planned on having the holidays with Mom and our son, Jeff in town. She was so happy to have us string up some outdoor lights along the front of the house in town and put a nice big tree in the front window. From a friend we had learned about these really neat timers for lights and heaters so we set up all the Christmas lights to go on and off automatically. This saved on electricity and kept Mom from having to remember to turn the lights off and on.

Then we had a thermostat that would turn on a red light in the front bedroom window of the house in town if the heat went out and the temperature dropped so that the neighbor across the street could call our heater technician. This made it much easier for us as it was not up to Mom to try to remember what to do in an emergency. After hearing about Mom locking herself out one day in the winter and the neighbor found mom sitting shivering on the front porch waiting for someone to help, we decided to leave a house key with that neighbor as well. That is when I found out that Mom had locked herself out during the summer but the bathroom window was open a little and that same neighbor had climbed in to unlock the door for Mom. Thankfully this very thoughtful neighbor was more than happy to help Mom and it made our life so much easier as well because it took away some of the worrisome parts of life with Mom. After Mom's stroke she had a bit of a problem with her memory circuits but we learned to work around that and make her feel very independent too.

Dealing with the many problems of aging parents was very interesting at times and also frustrating at other times. Most of the time we managed to make light of the situations and just laugh it off. Laughing made Mom happier too. It was sad to see Mom losing control and not remembering how to do things she had been doing forever. The worst one was Mom giving up her handcrafts because she could not remember how to do any of them. Now she had nothing but television to occupy herself. I had trouble holding my tongue at times when cleaning the house or yard and Mom would be hovering over me trying to tell me how to do things! She was a great supervisor and always had a lot of advice for me. Usually I would get Mom to singing some of the old time songs from the 40-50's which she enjoyed and knew all the words too, that gave me some peace. We are so very lucky to have had a Mom that was easy to get along with and seemed to be happy with so very little. Mom really loved her house and the neighborhood.

We were just thankful to have been able to give her a lovely place to spend the rest of her life.

Soon we were busy with a new year. Dick loved his job and was doing very well there. I was getting many things done out at our cabin and taking care of the house in town along with Mom. We were socializing with many friends on the river and feeling pretty good with our life. Dick was starting to talk about building a log work shop out behind the cabin for us. During the summer of 1986 we started clearing ground for the new shop and falling trees for the log walls. We had finished digging all the holes for the foundation pillars as we want all buildings at least four feet off the ground since we live on a river that can flood on occasion. I had painted two coats of preservatives on the logs pillars and we were about to put them in the ground. Our summer had been very busy and productive when the world seemed to fall apart.

Dick came home one evening and said that we needed to get everything up on high ground. It had been raining quite a bit and flooding was expected on the local rivers. Well, I had seen high water here before and was not surprised or afraid but the forecasters were talking serious flooding. So after putting our place in order we took the boat down the river and flew our airplane to town.

Mom was expecting us and had a wonderful dinner ready when we came to the house. We had a crazy evening watching TV and laughing at Mom, who had already seen the programs and knew what was going to happen, so she told us everything ahead of time! When we questioned her she said she had watched all these programs earlier in the day but loved seeing them again with us.

Since it was late we stayed overnight with Mom and early the next morning when I got up to get Dick off to work I found Mom still in bed. This was unusual as she liked to have the coffee on for Dick. I went in to see if she was sleeping and she was lying in a weird position so I touched her and her eyes popped open. Mom could not move anything but her eye lids and was gurgling like she was drowning. I yelled to Dick to call 911 because Mom has had a stroke or something and needs help NOW. I stayed with her and tried to make her more comfortable while waiting for the ambulance. Soon the EMT's were at the house and caring for Mom. They were so gentle and good to her. I was now scared about the condition Mom was in and could I bring her back to health again. I rushed to the hospital behind the ambulance and stayed with Mom as much as I could. She was in ICU and could only have one family visitor at a time. We finally found out that the aneurysm in Mom's head had burst and left her totally without any functions except movement of the eyelids. Even her eyes would not move, they were rolled to one side, and to talk to her I had to get on my knees so she could see me. Mom remained in the Intensive Care Unit for a week and many tests were done before the doctors told us that nothing more could be done for Mom as she had a very rare case of paralysis, only 156 known in the USA at the time. Trying to operate on her brain aneurysm would kill her so they were going to move her into a nursing home facility for custodial care only. I asked the doctors about Mom being on all those machines to stay alive and they told me to decide when to unplug the machines. Well that was like a punch in the stomach to me so I went in and talked to Mom to see if she understood what was to happen. It seems we could communicate with eye blinks for yes and no. Mom did not want to live in that condition so we made the decision to unplug the machines but to maintain fluids and the suctioning of her throat every 15 minutes. Mom was moved to the nursing home and her doctors said they were surprised that she did not die after being unplugged from the life support machines. Mom had a very strong heart and this was to keep her alive for awhile, even the doctors did not know exactly how long that would be.

In the meantime, we received word that our river had flooded big time and we had more than three feet of water going through our yard. This was a big concern for us because we still had the wringer washing machine and our snow machines on the ground plus one small shed that we stored our tools in.

After a few days I told Mom all about the flood and that Dick and I were going to make a quick trip up the river to check out our place for damages. So we drove our boat up, not knowing what the runway would look like we did not fly in, and found so much debris still flowing in the river. It was very harsh to see the damage to the river banks and so many trees washed down. When we arrived at our cabin there was still quite a bit of water in the low spots around the yard and everything else was covered with thick gooey silt. Our snow machines and washer had been underwater so we immediately washed them and flushed out the fuel. Then Dick lubricated the machines and ran them for a few minutes to get oil where it needed to be. Thankfully they all would continue to run for many years.

When we got around to opening our storage building we found all the electric tools had been under water. Dick told me to take them out to the river and sit there in the boat just swishing the tools up and down in the river water to clean the silt out of them. I said that seemed silly because everyone knows you don't put electric tools in water at which Dick replied, so what they have already been more than wet. The fast cleaning just might save some of the tools. Well, it did and to this day we are still using all various tools. Only one of the electric drills gave up eventually.

Anyway we spent about two days cleaning up our things and making some order out of the chaos at the cabin before returning to town. We had firewood still scattered through the woods but no time to collect it and put it back in piles. Our lumber that we had made with our chain saw mill and left drying with spacers had been picked up by the water and floated off into two places but still in the neat piles. We had never seen anything like this and laughed, which felt good inside.

I was quite anxious to see how Mom was doing and wanted to get back to town but nothing had changed. We were told that Mom may live in the same condition for many years and I felt so sorry for her. She cannot eat, talk or move any part of her body and this is not living. I started to hope for a quick and easy end for Mom, like going to sleep and never waking up. I would spend hours each day with Mom and even tried to get our son, Jeff, to visit at times. Her condition really frightened Jeff but I told him to just talk to her like normal telling about his days at work and play. So life continued with Mom never changing and the nurses had to vacuum her throat several times an hour to keep her from drowning in her own fluid. This created such rawness in her throat that gave her much pain so I asked that the pain be relieved so she can rest.

Now the bomb shell falls again as we get a call from Dick's mother. She is crying and very upset as she was diagnosed with breast cancer and due to go into surgery in a few days. Since I am the one who has always taken care of her when needed she wanted me to be with her now. Dick said we should both fly south on an airline and be with his mother. I had to agree even though I was pulled to stay in Fairbanks with my Mom. Dick's mother and father had taken my younger brother and me in to live with them for a year before Dick and I were married. She was always there with us for all the holidays and so much more. So I went to talk to my mother about this and asked her what I should do. Should I stay or go to California for a week or two. My mother agreed I should go and would see her when I get back. Our son, Jeff, agreed to visit his grandmother each day and she also had friends from church going by to see her so Mom was not totally alone.

My mother only lived for eleven days after being put into the nursing home. I was fixing dinner at my mother-in-laws shortly after arriving there when I had the sudden urge to telephone my Mom. The nurse there held the telephone to Mom's ear and I was able to tell her about Dick's mother and her surgery. I told my Mom how much I missed her and loved her before the nurse said she had to hang up. About 45 minutes later on September 16, 1986 the nursing home called me to let me know that my mother had just passed away. Oh, I was feeling so guilty for not being there with her but no one expected that to happen.

Before all this happened Mom and I had thoroughly discussed death and what she expected in her future. I made sure that before I left Fairbanks I had made arrangements for Mom to be cremated after death and had paid the fees in full. So now I called the Funeral Home to go pick up Mom and I would pick up her ashes when I came home to Fairbanks. Dick and I had planned to take Mom's ashes on our next trip south and deposit them in the California desert where she wanted to be. It is always nice thinking that Mom is pushing up those lovely desert primroses there. Then we had to call other family members to let them know about Mom's death.

When we arrived home in Fairbanks we wondered just what we should do with the house we were buying that Mom had been living in and decided to keep making payments and just wait for a while to see if Dick's mother would need our help soon. Thankfully that was a good decision because Dick's mother had a stroke as a complication from her surgery and was now in a rehabilitation center in Santa Barbara, California. Her sister, Jessie was helping her and staying with her at this time.

Oh, I almost forgot to mention that during all of these problems with our mothers, the flooding and all, I had a medical problem and was diagnosed with a tumor the size of a grapefruit. The doctor wanted to do surgery ASAP. I was scheduled to have surgery on the day before Christmas 1986 and would go home four days later. As it turned out I wound up with a complete hysterectomy but after testing the tumor was not cancerous. I did have a long incision down my belly and would spend many weeks to total recovery.

In January 1987 Dick was being sent down to Oklahoma City for another FAA school that was to last about two months. We had decided to drive our own vehicle out and would stop to visit our son, Robert, and his family on the way to Oklahoma. So only two weeks after my surgery we were on the road in a terrific snow storm headed south. In fact, the snow storm lasted all the way into Oklahoma City where they had a record breaking 12 inches of snow! I was sure glad that we had a Chevy suburban four wheel drive because it made driving so much easier. Dick put the back seats down and made a big bed for us to sleep in. I would climb over the front seat back into the bed area and sleep off and on during the whole trip. This helped in my recovery from surgery.

When we were visiting our son and his family in Bremerton, Washington we saw that the big Seattle Boat show was going on over the weekend in the Seattle King Dome so the six of us, Robert, Tina, Jeffrey, Crystalynn, Dick and I, drove over to look around for the day. This was very tiring for me so soon after my surgery but they had a lot of seating where I could rest now and then. Anyway, Dick and I had found a beautiful aluminum modified v-hull jet boat with all the bells and whistles that we wanted. So we gathered all the information and then continued on our journey to Oklahoma City.

A few days after arriving in Oklahoma City we called the Duckworth Boat company in Clarkston, Washington and asked if they could have our dream boat ready for us to pick up on our way back north in March. After several telephone calls and giving them all the specs we wanted we came upon an agreement for price and pick up date near the end of March. Well, we were very excited now and worked hard at getting the best financing we could so that all this would come together without a hitch.

Dick finished his schooling and we drove over to California to see how his mother was doing before we headed back north to our home in Alaska. Mom J. was in a wheel chair and learning to use a walker. She decided she wanted to move up with us so we took her in the suburban for the drive north. When we made a side trip over to Clarkston, Washington to pick up our new boat Mom J. was shocked to see how big it really was and that we planned to tow it home in the snow and over icy roads. The boat was about 24 feet long on the trailer and the company had fixed it up with carpeting covering the windshield and the leading edges of the trailer to prevent damage from flying gravel off the roadways. We had purchased a complete mooring cover for the boat which was on it for transporting as well. So after signing the paperwork, picking up a check at the local bank and paying for the boat we headed north. We thought it was really odd how we just bought a boat and never saw the actual people involved or the bank personnel that were carrying our loan. All of this through telephone calls and faxed paperwork! Even the boat payments would be automatically withdrawn from our checking account each month. I would send extra money as I could to pay it off as soon as possible.

Our trip back north went very well. The biggest problem was getting Mom in and out of the car which sat fairly high off the ground so Dick made a two foot square box that was about eight inches high. This box gave us a better leverage for moving Mom into and out of the car. We drove long hours through the days and stopped at various roadhouses at night.

Pretty soon we had a routine worked out and managed to move through the days like normal. Along the way somewhere we stopped and bought some moon boots for Mom. When we finally discovered that Mom was getting very cold in the back seat even with a blanket for her legs we moved her to the front seat and I sat in the back. This worked out much better for Mom and she couldn't seem to get enough hot air circulation in the back when the temperatures dropped to 30 below zero and colder. I think she was amazed that we were even surviving in those temperatures!

We had some great laughs when stopping for the night as almost every roadhouse had a special soup of the day which Mom usually chose. It seemed to be split pea soup, so we joked that a big truck was ahead of us delivering split peas to all the restaurants along the highway. The last straw was a stop at the first open lodge in Alaska and the waitress said that split pea soup was their special of the day. The three of us were laughing so hard we couldn't even explain to the waitress why. The waitress just left us alone for a few minutes until we could get ourselves together and make a dinner order.

As we neared the Alaska border Mom was getting very upset and when we asked her why she told us she was afraid that the United States would not let her back into the country. This was because she was not a US citizen and still held a green card as a British Citizen after living in America since 1927. We tried to get her to relax and assured her that she would not be stopped. Mom never relaxed until we were clear of the border and into Alaska by a few miles!

Having Dick's Mom with us now made it easier for the transition on the death of my mother whom we had been taking care of for almost four years. We still miss the happiness my mother brought into a room and all the laughs we shared over the silliest things. I know that she knew how very much we loved her.

Now I hope to be able to make life good and as happy as possible for Mom J. She seems to be very satisfied with the house in town. Soon we were able to get her settled into a routine of life in the cold north country.

Chapter 15

A New Challenge

Dick's mother was so surprised to see the lovely home we had in Fairbanks for her to live in. A couple of months after settling in to the area Mom assured us that she wanted to stay with us. We had not been sure that this move was going to work for Mom so we decided to do a couple of months of trial first. After that time went by, Mom and I made a commercial flight back to California to close out her apartment and send some of her things up to Alaska. This is a very tough job to close out the independent lifestyle of a parent. When I cleaned out all the closets, cupboards and such Mom selected some things to save that we shipped to Fairbanks. This process brought out many stories from Mom about different times in her life. It was fun to listen to her stories and learn more of her family history. Since we only had ten days to complete our task I worked while Mom talked to me and we had a big yard sale that weekend. I was able to sell most of Mom's things giving her a nice nest egg for her savings account.

Many of the neighbors came by during the yard sale to chat with Mom which made her feel so good. It was funny to hear Mom bragging about her house and life in Alaska to these old neighbors. I think the new lifestyle and adventure added some spice to Mom's life that was very good for her.

Before we left Santa Barbara we stayed overnight with Aunt Jessie, Mom's sister, who had been very close to Mom since Jessie moved to the USA from Scotland in 1958. I told Aunt Jessie that we had a large home with three bedrooms and she was welcome to come live with Mom in Fairbanks where they could maintain some independence and still be close. This was met with an emphatic,

"NO, I am not moving to any cold country thank you." Still I told her the offer would stand forever and she was always welcome even if only to visit for a while during the warm summer months. Aunt Jessie never took advantage of this opportunity and never even visited Alaska.

Once a year Mom would want to fly down and spend a month with her sister or go visit her daughter, Joyce in Georgia. Since she was afraid to fly unattended I would fly with her helping with all her needs and then turn around and return home while Mom stayed for a month. If she went to see Joyce then I only made one trip and Joyce would return with Mom. This was difficult and costly but Mom paid for the airline tickets so we did it her way.

Soon Mom informed us that she wanted to go to the cabin with us all the time because she did not like being alone so much in Fairbanks. At this point Dick and I quickly made some ramps for our river boat. The ramps were made from ¾ inch plywood cut into two pieces 2x8 foot with one inch angle iron screwed to the long sides making a curb for the chair wheels. Then we made a short ramp to get the wheel chair from the top of the boat engine compartment down to the deck between the front seats. By using the side of the boat against the river bank we were able to load and unload Mom much easier. Now we could get Mom aboard in her wheel chair and also off the boat up the river bank at the cabin. This started Mom on coming to the cabin with us all the time and that didn't work either because she wanted me to just sit in the cabin with her. I needed to get some fresh air and space now and then, plus Dick and I had many projects going on that required my help. So there were times when we made the trip up river alone and left Mom in town with a caretaker looking in on her.

So you can see by this time we established a new routine in life with Dick's mother living in the house in Fairbanks and we would be there three days a week. Mom would come to the cabin with us often but we had many times we went alone. We would even dress Mom in a snow suit, parka and boots for ride in our double wide snow machine in the winter time to the cabin. She seemed to love the trip up the winter trail and the fresh air was good for her. We were so glad to have that double wide machine (Skidoo Bombardier) with the bucket seats so we could seat belt Mom in and wrap her legs with a blanket. Mom's biggest complaint was she had to wear a full face mask to protect her from frostbite and she hated having her face covered. We even managed to get her into our airplane for trips during the summer and winter. She loved the airplane and the boat rides on the river too.

One time after landing in the plane during the fall, after our boat was put away for the winter, we had to use our canoe to get across the river from the runway to the cabin. Dick and I crossed first so I could catch the canoe when Mom was brought over. Mom insisted on helping Dick paddle so he gave her a paddle and they come across to me. As they were crossing Mom kept leaning over to one side and Dick was sure they were going to tip over. We just could not convince Mom how important it was to sit up straight and when told to sit up she would lean the other way. I was sure that the canoe would capsize and both of them would wind up in the water. Sometimes Mom got into some precarious positions and never even knew it but she was having fun and still living life well into her late eighties.

Another time in the winter as we were taking off from the frozen river in the airplane on skis we kept getting gusts of wind causing us to climb a little and then drop a little for the first mile. During this time Dick kept good control of the plane and using ground effect we finally were safely airborne and able to climb out over the trees. Dick made the comment that ignorance is bliss, after looking at Mom in the back seat as happy as a lark not knowing how tricky the take off had been.

I still did all the housework and laundry at the town house. By now I had hired a young boy about 12 or 13 years old to keep up the yard work. Eric was terrific and treated our home like it was his taking care of things even if we were not around. Like pulling the dead flowers and cleaning up the flower beds in the fall, fertilizing when needed and watering the yard twice a week. In the fall he would drain and store our water hose. Eric would even shovel the driveway if we were not around and have his mother drive in and out of the driveway making tracks so it was not obvious that we were gone. You couldn't have asked for a better and more thorough yard care person. We were sure to give him a good bonus at the holidays too.

Dick's mother required a lot more care than my mother had, so I had to spend more time with her. The hardest parts were getting her in and out of the bath even though we had previously installed all the necessary hand rails and such. Mom J. would not do much to try to help herself. We did get her to using only the walker around inside the house. I bought a tall bar stool for Mom to use in the kitchen so she could sit and work at the sink or stove. This helped her some but it was also the down fall of Mom's health.

Mom had the habit of not sitting carefully but just plopping down in a chair. Sometimes she would not even look behind her to see if the chair was there. This caused a few unnecessary falls with her usually landing awkwardly in the recliner chair in the living room. We would continually remind her to be careful and look before sitting down. On one of her famous falls from the stool in the kitchen she broke a hip and was hospitalized for a while following surgery. Thankfully I was there in the kitchen with her at the time and could summon help. Then we were back to physical therapy trying to get her as mobile as possible. This accident seemed to be the end of Mom's spirit and she became very depressed. Her medications were making her feel a bit better and she was definitely easier to get along with now but the side effects from all the medicine was taking a toll.

Soon we were back to a more normal home routine and now I would be sure and do ALL of the cooking leaving meals ready to heat and serve for Mom. There was a small microwave oven in the kitchen and all Mom had to do was put her meal in to heat and then eat. I was always sure to have her favorite snack items on hand too. By this time I had discovered the local Hospice so I was able to get various ladies to come in and help Mom in the mornings with taking her medications on the days that we were gone up the river to the cabin. This gave us a bit of breathing space which is greatly needed when caring for ones parents.

It wasn't long before we discovered that Mom was not eating correctly and living on toast, soup or cereal when we were not in town with her because she couldn't be bothered to heat her meal. Then she thought we were trying to starve her. So I made arrangements for a hospice lady to come twice a day when I was not there to be sure Mom had breakfast and her medications in the morning, then a warm dinner at night. I asked the hospice lady to just be sure than Mom ate by sitting at the table with her. I still prepared all the meals and had them set up like frozen dinners that only needed to be micro-waved for a few minutes. I would bake cookies and other goodies that I knew Mom liked for treats which were easy for her to get on her own. This worked for a while until Mom decided she did not want to open the door for anyone to come in. So I gave the hospice lady a key to let herself in and she would find Mom in bed when ever she came. Now I was concerned about Mom's mental stability and tried to get her out each day for a wheel chair ride about the mall. Mom would not go to church, didn't want to be a part of any senior citizen organization and did not try to talk with any neighbors. This was not good behavior and very anti-social. I asked Mom many times if she was sorry she came to Alaska or if she wanted to live someplace else. Mom always said that this was a good place for her and we treated her well so we put her feelings down to depression. We were also noticing some dementia now, or Alzheimer's disease. The doctor assured us it was progressing quite slowly and not to worry at this time.

Life continued to run fairly smoothly after we figured out how to cope with everything. Dick's sister, Joyce, came to visit Mom in Fairbanks a couple of times and seemed to be pleased with our arrangement as well. After about four years Mom one day said she wanted to move into a nursing home because she was becoming too much of a burden. We assured her that she was not a burden but she insisted. We let a couple of days pass to be sure she knew what she wanted and then she started talking about wanting to be in a warmer climate possibly near her daughter, Joyce. Well this set the research in motion for various assisted living and nursing homes around Alaska, and near Joyce. It was far too expensive here in Alaska for Mom's income and even if we helped her some we still could not afford the care facilities here. In the meantime, Joyce found a few places near her home in Georgia, so we flew down with Mom to go look at them. We were all very pleased with one of them and proceeded to make arrangements for Mom to move in there. Even this place, which reminded us of the movie DRIVING MISS DAISY because of the elegant setting, was going to use all of Mom's income plus $500 a month from us and another $500 a month from Joyce. We never told Mom that we would be supplementing her income because that would make her feel terrible.

Eventually move in day came and we were there to settle Mom in with some of her photos on the walls and other things of hers to make it feel like home. She managed to live in three different places over the remaining six years of her life. Joyce would visit her often and we would see Mom once a year or more. She loved to be taken out on a drive and have lunch at McDonalds when we were visiting. In 1996 both Mom and Joyce made a big move from Georgia to Boulder, Colorado. Mom was living not far from Joyce's new home. We even managed to get her out several days to a family reunion which was her last one. Most of her grandchildren and great-grandchildren were there making it a special moment.

Mom died only a few months after that and was cremated following her request. We later spread her ashes along with her oldest daughter's ashes at sea from our sailboat. We didn't have the whole family with us but Dick, Joyce, our niece Kathy, our son Robert and I tried to do the best we could as a memorial. That is what Mom wanted. I think when you follow through on your parent's final wishes it doesn't matter what you do but it just feels better and right.

When Dick and I came home, after Mom had moved into the assisted living place in Georgia, we were thinking very hard about trying to retire by the end of May 1994. We kept the house in town for a year and finally decided that we could not afford to hang on to the house and retire so it was best to sell the house now and cut our losses. Yes, the housing market had really dropped since we purchased the house so we would have to sell it for less than we paid. There was no indication of the market rising in the near future and the payments would keep us from retiring soon so we listed the house and proceeded to sell it losing about $40,000. In hindsight, which is always very clear, we would have been better off just renting a home for our mothers since we only had a need for a house over six years in Fairbanks. When we knew the house was definitely sold I had a big yard sale and sold everything from the house except a few personal items we wanted to save. We were so happy that our dear friend, Ruthie, wanted the dishes and kitchen ware and we remember my Mom every time we eat over at Ruth's house now. The single mother with two children that bought the house needed furniture, so many items were purchased by her.

We kept one queen size bed and dresser from the house that we moved into one of the bedrooms at our friends John and Judy Vogt's house in town so we had a place to stay if we wanted to spend a few days in town. This arrangement worked very well for us for a couple of years. Then we wound up putting that bed and dresser into one of the motel rooms at the Salcha River Lodge where we spent some time during freeze up and break up for a couple of years. We really enjoyed spending time with our dear friends Art and Jean Thompson who owned the lodge. It was a real pleasure to even help out at busy times at the lodge where we managed to get to know many of the local residents who lived along the highway.

Once again we were living alone and full time on the river which had always been our goal. Sometimes you run into all sorts of challenges before reaching a goal. By this time many of our river neighbors had moved into town so the abundant winter socializing and holiday parties dwindled. We still had the normal summer barbecues on the long holiday weekends which are always great fun and a time to visit with neighbors. Of course, we still had our dear friends and neighbors, Rose and Roger Anderson, along with Michael Grant that were permanent river residents. About this time you could see big changes in life on the river. Things were quieting down and the big parties were fewer as people matured and started thinking about retirements.

One time when Dick was hurt and had his arm in a cast we had a couple, Dick and Ellen, come by to fall trees and peal logs for our generator shed. There is a certain time span in which this job should be done to make it easier. Dick and Ellen just showed up and said, "What trees do you want cut?" The next thing we knew the job was done as Dick Deweese fell and cut trees into lengths, Ellen and I pealed the logs and soon a pile of logs were sitting in our yard. Now that was really something special. We will never forget them.

Our friend, Ruth, was running the Salcha Post Office before the Parras bought the Lodge and we had so much fun with her and husband Matt after he bought her a snow machine and she learned to travel up the river. They wound up purchasing some property about 15 miles below us on the river and built a nice cabin there. Matt worked for the FAA, along with Dick, and he would ride snow machines up the river often with another friend, Leroy, for the weekend. They would stop at our cabin for a meal or just a snack with coffee. We always enjoyed their visits and after several years we met Matt's wife, Ruth, who became one of my best friends here. Together we enjoyed many salmon fishing trips, hunting trips, snow machine trips and just having them visit us at our cabin.

Ruth and I would dry fruits for the winters and share our gardening tips. I learned to do some pottery work with her as she had a small business selling Alaskan clay items she made. Our grand-daughters have little girl tea sets made by Ruth using Alaskan clay that we dug up ourselves along the Knik River bed.

One thing that never changed on the river was you always knew that when you needed help all your river neighbors would be there. I have never been around such a wonderful, helpful group of people that are closer at times than even family. Maybe that is because most of us are living so far from all our families we seem to flock together.

There are so many people who have helped to make our life very pleasant here on the Salcha River. We have been given rides back up to our cabin after pulling our boat each fall, thanks to Jim Hill, Roger and Betty Redfern, and John Sauer for these rides.

Other neighbors have dropped off our mail many times or shared in their bounty from the seas and woods.

We have had machinery break downs that required getting parts, even a full engine one time for the boat, that have been delivered right to us at the cabin by one of our neighbors. John Binkley even flew a new starter to us in his helicopter this last fall. Now that was going way beyond being helpful and we will remember his forever.

There are far too many stories like the above to mention them all but we do extend a very grateful thank you to our many friends and neighbors for their help, concern for us and just being there for us when needed. We love each and every one of you.

Chapter 16

BOATING ADVENTURES

When we first started boating here in Alaska we owned a small open flat bottom 16 foot Jon boat with a 40 horsepower Mercury outboard engine. After a couple years in freezing cold rains while running the river we started to modify our little boat. Using plywood we constructed a windscreen across the front with a Lexan windshield which really helped a lot. We could even have lawn chairs in the boat for more comfort right behind the windshield, except for the driver who was stuck out in the back at the tiller handle. The next thing we did was construct a framework to hold a canvas top so we could be free of the down pouring rain. Now we felt like we were traveling in style and so much more comfortable too! Then along came some very high water one summer when our boat was tied up to the riverbank and a tree floating down the river caught the boat top and ripped the whole thing off. We found pieces of the plywood windshield and top off in the woods all busted up where it had been deposited by the flood waters. So much for boating comfort now! We never rebuilt a windshield for that boat.

As we stated in the beginning Dick hardly drove our boat as long as we had two sons living at home because they really loved the adventure of driving anything! Sometimes the water would be so low that the engine would touch bottom and jump up, cavitating, or sucking air. We have been known to drive the boat onto a shallow submerged gravel bar when the river was muddy or the sun glaring in your face. During these times if the boat actually stopped we would get out and push the boat back into deeper water. Often the boat just slid across the small areas and we were back on your our way without so much as a flinch.

Dick was always teaching someone in the family to drive the

boat by sitting along side and just letting go. Dick would quietly give directions and point out why you would be turning this way or that way to avoid some hazard like a snag under water, rocks or a sweeper leaning over the river. We called this learning to read the river. But I think that I probably hold the record for the dumbest maneuver ever. I was learning to handle the outboard tiller handle as we made a trip up river to visit friends. It seemed to me that the tiller was always turning the opposite direction that I wanted it to so our path over the water was very erratic. Soon we were met head on by a very fast inboard jet boat leaving a large wake in the water. Dick instructed me to do something and I thought I felt his hand take the tiller so I just let go! Now at 30 mph when the tiller went over to one side, that sudden spin around in the middle of the river was exciting for sure! Thankfully no one was hurt and we never hit anything. Dick grabbed the tiller then and asked if I wanted it back to which I replied, "No, not right now." Our sons were laughing so hard I thought they would split a gut but I did not think it was that funny! Eventually I did learn to run the boat by myself.

Try to imagine driving at 30 mph in a pouring rain without a windshield. Those little raindrops can really sting on your face. It is very hard to keep your eyes open too. We would use goggles but then you couldn't see very well through the blurred lenses so we always removed the goggles before long and just endured the stinging raindrops. Even wearing huge rubber ponchos we usually wound up a little wet by the time we reached the highway but that never slowed us down. In the late fall we would be riding in the boat wearing lightweight insulated coveralls and gloves to keep warm.

Each year the river changes in many places creating new channels or even new bigger log jams that you must find a way around. Sometimes you are moving along and make a turn in the river which is like a blind corner and find yourself in the wrong place moving quite fast. This usually happens during the first runs in the spring after changes have been made from the winter ice going out or following a flood. In times like these you put the boat into reverse and try to turn around before you hit anything. We have had a few close calls doing this maneuver but have never swamped a boat.

One time we took a bit of water over the side and Dick told me to remove the drain plug. Well, I thought he had just lost his mind because we were still moving along on the river in fairly deep water but he kept telling me that the fast moving boat would suction out the water in the hull. All I could see was us making a big hole in the boat which would help it sink faster! Dick finally just moved in and pulled the drain plug as I was too scared to do that job. It was astonishing to see the water all completely drain from our boat and then Dick replaced the plug. I just could not believe what I was seeing. It seems that I am always learning something new from my husband and many times I think he is absolutely crazy when he tells me of his plans! Oh well, I always knew that life would never be boring with Dick and he makes sure that holds true.

Then in 1987 we bought a new boat which had all our dream items like a closed cabin with a heater, windshield wipers, shock mounted seats and so much more. We felt like real royalty in this boat. After towing our new boat, a 22 foot Duckworth inboard jet, almost 2500 miles from the state of Washington in March 1987, we found out by trial and error just how different boats can handle on the water. We were use to the old Jon boat sliding out on turns and had learned to compensate for the slide but when we tried that in the Duckworth on the first very tight narrow corner we almost ran off the river on the inside of the turn. The Duckworth doesn't slide out and cuts the water quite nicely which put us in a precarious position very fast. It was very interesting to relearn how to drive a boat and I loved the steering wheel driving just like a car, instead of the tiller handle. After a couple of trips we were so happy with the new boat performance we would never go back to the Jon boat except for playing around fishing now and then.

We kept the old Jon boat for a few years pulled out on the river bank at our cabin but it seemed a waste to not have the boat used. Eventually, we sold that Jon boat to our friend Ruthie and her husband Matt. Matt proceeded to sink the boat on his very first trip from our house down the river to their cabin losing his gun and other items. We felt bad about his loses but he did not follow the path we had shown him to run the boat down river. That was really a pilot error that cost him. Thankfully both Matt and Ruth came out alright even if a little wet. After getting a radio call about the sinking we took our new boat to the spot and helped to recover the sunken boat and motor but we never found Matt's gun. Our grandson swept the area for over an hour with a long poled fish net trying to latch onto a gun or other valuables under the murky waters.

It did not take us long to become so accustom to the Duckworth and to this day we still feel like royalty when riding around in that boat. It was such a big change to have a completely closed in boat cabin with a heater for the colder days and even windshield wipers for the rain. Dick put side view mirrors on the boat and we installed a Citizen Band radio with a 13 foot whip antenna, so we had communications with our home and other people on the river. Then Dick built an intercom system so that we could wear good aircraft headsets and be able to talk in normal tones over the engine sound. The intercom would always give preference to the CB radio transmissions so we never missed a message or emergency. Dick also installed a good marine am-fm radio so we could listen to the local radio stations while riding on the river. Nothing like sitting back relaxing while listening to some good music as you enjoyed the travels up and down a beautiful scenic river.

We always keep survival gear in the boat, which is stored under our back bench seats. This included a first aid kit, good foul weather suits, chest waders, shovel, chain saw winch, a hand come-along, two oak wheel barrow handles for pry bars and a tree cutting chain saw. Our fishing poles and tackle box are always with us. Several feet of rope, plastic tarps, propane camp cook stove with pans and a two gallon jug of drinking water added for comfort. Then we carried the usual things like paper towels, toilet paper, window cleaner, flashlights and even a large spot light. We keep two sleeping bags in stuff bags which we used as extra arm rests on the back bench seats. Now this sounds like a lot of stuff but we have had many times over the years that we were thankful we were prepared to stay out overnight along the river due to mechanical break downs, ice or flooding and even thick fog. Sometimes we just enjoyed a quick camp out up the river somewhere for fun.

Our boat is equipped with a swim platform on the back and when our grandchildren were visiting us they loved to have us take the boat in to a calm slough with deep water and sandy bottom, just a couple of miles above our cabin. The children enjoyed many hours of diving off the front of the anchored boat to swim around and climb up the back of the boat to repeat the process. Dick and I would even swim with them sometimes. Our river water temperatures never get much above 36-38 degrees even in the summer!

I remember one time we were so glad to have that swim platform off the back of the boat because it saved Dick's life. We were coming up the river for the first time in the spring on May 10th at about 10am when we encountered a three-quarter mile long ice jam from bank to bank. So we pulled into a quiet slough that had plenty of water and proceeded to wait for the ice jam to move out. By 10pm the ice jam had still not budged so we decided to just make up our bed with the bench seats and pull out the sleeping bags until morning. Dick and I had been to town to get groceries and other supplies so we had a huge boat load. I had fixed us some dinner which we enjoyed while watching the bits of ice break loose and flow away.

The terrific sounds that come from an ice jam are mind boggling, so much scraping, crunching, grinding and even tinkling sounds like chimes. The ice floes can be stacked several feet high in multiple layers and have so much power to destroy anything in its path. It is really an awesome experience to watch the ice go out after a long winter. We felt very safe tucked into a good slough out of the main channel of water.

Just as I was climbing into my sleeping bag Dick told me to get up and watch the fantastic show as the ice was really moving out. Both of us stood on top of the engine compartment for a better view and within seconds our boat started to rise from the increase in water, even in the slough. Then just as quickly the water started down very fast and Dick ran forward to start the engine while I untied our shoreline. Before we were able to move even one boat length backwards we were left sitting high and dry in very gooey mud. It was amazing to see the water more than 600 feet from our boat! We instantly started the process of pushing, winching and doing whatever was necessary to get our boat back into water. Dick and I worked until after 1am but we were both so tired by then that we were making stupid errors. It was time to tie the boat to the shore, quit working and go to bed for a few hours. So that is just what we did.

After a good sleep we were up and ready to tackle the project of getting our boat back to water again. At this time in the morning the ice near the edge of the river had refrozen to the bottom of the riverbed. It did not take much time to get the winch rigging all set up to move the boat and when Dick first started to use the winch the boat slid very easily over the frozen river bottom. We laughed at how easy this job was turning out to be, as we moved our boat the rest of the 600 feet into the water once again. There was a long slab of ice holding firm between us and the main river channel but Dick was sure we could just drive towards it and slide across the ice back into the main channel on the other side. So after we had our equipment stowed away and the boat engine running we turned the boat around and gave it full throttle as we headed right up onto the slab of ice. The boat was sliding very nicely and we were excited about making this work for us when we came to a halt with the bow barely touching the edge of the ice at the main river channel of water. Dick turned off the engine. Gads, only one boat length from being back in the main river channel but it felt like miles! Our boat is very heavy and we had quite a load of supplies making it heavier still so this was not to be easy now because we are more out in the middle of the river with nowhere to hook a winch to pull ourselves. So Dick climbed out the back of the boat with one of our wooden wheel barrow handles and proceeded to see if he could pry the boat off the ice. Well the boat started to move right away and Dick kept prying until the boat slid into the water and he was able to just step right onto the back of the boat. This mornings round of work only took about an hour total and we had our boat floating.

Both of us let out a big yell of a success and Dick tried to start the motor again. Nothing happened so I was using the key to start the motor and Dick had the engine compartment open to see why it would not run. We had fuel and spark but the actual starter was doing nothing but a clunk. Now we are drifting backwards down the river among the many small icebergs that kept banging into the hull. Dick swore a little and ran forward to deploy the anchor to get us stopped before we hit a tree or went aground. After a couple of tosses the anchor held fast to the river bottom. Now Dick had time to check out the starter and when he finally had it disconnected we found the inside was nothing but a bunch of blackened bits of metal ground up. We were not going anywhere without that starter working.

As we were contemplating our problem we heard a boat coming up the river and thought we would have some help real soon. Finally we could see the boat coming with the early morning sunrise hitting the boat head on. The couple who were riding in the boat so concentrated on missing all the icebergs and floating debris that they passed right by us and never even saw us. Of course we were waving and hollering but a voice cannot be heard over most boat engines. We started laughing as they proceeded to drive off into the sunrise. Then their boat wake started cutting loose the shelf ice along the river bank and it was floating down the river banging into our boat. We tried to fend off the ice with our wooden wheel barrow handles and managed to do a pretty good job for a few minutes. Then our anchor broke loose and we were back to free floating backward in the main current with a lot of ice flowing too.

The next problem was to get our boat over to the river bank where we could tie up to shore and wait for someone to come along in another boat. Dick told me to move to the back so I could fend off any sweepers, trees leaning across the water from the bank, and keep them from hitting the boat.

Dick went forward again and pulled the anchor and would toss it to the side so he could pull our boat sideways across the river channel. He repeated this process several times until we could almost touch shore and the boat was really slowed down now. I grabbed onto a sweeper and was holding the boat firm as Dick tried to throw our anchor up into a leaning tree to make us stable and safe. The first toss of the anchor missed and I couldn't hold onto the tree much longer when Dick told me to let go, so I did. Well, that was not good as the tree swept right over our boat cabin and struck Dick in the back pushing him overboard into the freezing water. All I heard was "HELP" and a splash! Now I was scared because I could not see Dick anywhere. I hollered for him and he answered while sticking up one hand as he floated alongside the boat hull. At this time we were both concerned about getting him out of the water. Dick managed to get a hold onto the back of our boat but with clothes filled with water and ice he did not have the strength to pull himself up onto our swim platform. I ran to him and grabbed both his straps at the top of his overalls and yelled pull as I pulled as hard as I could. Working together we did get him onto the boat and he ran forward again asking, "Are we having fun yet?" Now we are both cracking up with laughter as Dick grabs the anchor for the last time, as this toss landed up in a tree and we were holding tight. Then I asked him just how we were supposed to get that anchor out of the tree and he said, "Who cares at least we are out of danger at the moment!" When Dick was able to pause for a moment I asked him if he would like some dry clothes to put on. Thankfully I had just purchased some new work clothes for him on our trip to town so he could get dry and warm again.

While Dick was getting changed into dry clothing I made a cell phone call to town to see if anyone we knew was coming up the river today. We located a neighbor who was just getting ready to leave town and asked if he would pick up a new starter for us and bring it up the river. Now that was just great luck and we were happy to know that our luck was finally changing for the day. Our neighbor did not know exactly when he would be here but we told him that was not a problem as we were not going anywhere and were settled quite warm and happy at the moment.

This was a beautiful sunny day, the birds were singing profusely and the flowing river ice was fascinating to watch. I asked Dick if he would like to join me in a picnic on the back of the boat in the sunshine. So that is just what we did while laughing and discussing our little adventure on the water. This was one time we left the highway on the morning of May 10th and did not get to our cabin until the evening of May 11th.

There are many times of overloading the boat and then having trouble getting it on step to run up the river. Dick would ask me to go sit right out on the bow for better weight balance until we were moving good on the water then I could return to the inside of the boat for the trip home. At these times one never stopped for anything until we were at home. One day we had been loading sheets of metal roofing on the boat to haul up for the new house we were building. I don't remember exactly how many sheets we had but when loading them two at a time they were quite light. Our stack of roofing was only about 12-18 inches high of 3x12 foot sheets of metal. Well, no matter how hard we tried the boat wouldn't plane correctly on the water so we went back to the landing and off loaded about half of the roofing for a second trip. Sometimes we waste more time trying to make fewer trips but we do get a lot of exercise and laughs along the way.

We are not the only ones to have these types of experiences or fun. Many people who travel the rivers in Alaska have some great tales of survival. I remember one year when we were flying to our cabin and followed the river to see how the ice was doing during break up. We came across four air boats (common swamp running vessels in the south) that were trying to get up the river and had been stopped by an ice jam. One boat was on the upriver side of the jam going around in circles trying to find an open channel of water to continue his journey. The other three air boats were moving across a gravel bar and trying to find a way back to the water while running through the willows. Dick and I circled overhead a few times trying to point out the direction of travel for them but that was not working. So we continued on home to our cabin. We learned later that they gave up and had started a small fire on the ice to cook some hot dogs when suddenly the ice gave way and their fire and hot dogs went with it. This did open the channel for them and they completed their trip up the river. Everyone was very happy but still hungry!

One mid-summer day when Dick and I were coming up the river in our boat we spotted a lot of camp gear floating in the river. We stopped to pull out sleeping bags, ice chest and a waterproof case with a rifle. Now we were very concerned about finding bodies floating too and kept a sharp eye out for anything. Soon we rounded a bend in the river and saw two men walking along the bank so we stopped to ask if they had a problem. The men replied, "Didn't you see our boat?" When we answered no, they could not believe this and proceeded to tell us what happened. It seems that one man was selling his air boat and was giving a test ride to the new buyer. For some unknown reason their engine had quit in a very bad spot with a heavy current and several sweepers along the bank. The boat floated back into the sweepers which instantly swamped their boat and it sunk in seconds. Dick and I went back to find the boat and sure enough it was sitting on the engine cage on the river bottom with the bow barely sticking out of the water by a couple of inches. It was easy to pass by the 16 foot long boat and not see it. Anyway, we gave the two men the gear we had found floating in the river which made them feel a little better. Especially the new boat owner who had brought his brand new $1500 rifle with him, which had never been fired yet, and the gun was still dry and OK.

Dick and I like to use our boat for fall camping trips way up the middle fork of the Salcha River. It was always an adventure just getting to the spot to camp. With our new boat we camped right inside the boat as the back seats made into a double bed and the covered cabin served as our tent. I would set up my cooking area on top of the engine compartment in the back and we would be just as snug as a bug in a rug. This was really great when it was pouring rain. I would stay with boat and Dick would take hikes during the day looking for moose so we would have our winter meat. Often we camped near beaver houses as it was fun to watch their activities. On this one trip we were tied up near a beaver house alongside the river bank. During the early morning hours, about 5am, we heard an odd noise and when Dick sat up to look we had a grizzly bear right at the bow of our boat. Well, this is quite a shock coming out of a dead sleep and when Dick tried to reach his rifle his mummy sleeping bag tossed him back down. This happened twice before he finally got the zipper open so he could reach the rifle. I woke up to the sound of Dick's voice saying, "BEAR, BEAR, BEAR!" I sat up and proceeded to talk quietly to the bear, who was only about six feet from me, saying he should go away as it was too early in the morning and we had not even brushed our teeth yet. I mumbled on and on about anything until I finally bored the poor bear to death and he just walked away. About this time my husband was laughing so hard at me because he said that he couldn't believe my reaction to being awakened by a grizzly bear so close. Dick asked me what I thought I was doing and I told him I just wanted that bear to know that we did not appreciate his interruptions one bit. Dick said any normal woman would have screamed but not his wife. That is probably true but then that kind of woman would not be married to Dick. We both thought that bear was huge as he stood on his hind legs looking us over but after we were dressed and could go look at his tracks we found he was not big at all, probably a three year old. When one is excited and sleepy things look out of proportion, anyway that is our excuse and we are sticking to it.

We had our grandchildren stay with us for several weeks during many summers and of course one of the big things with them was going for boat rides and fishing. Dick had taught all three grandchildren how to drive the boat and that was a great past time for them. Our grandson seems to have a problem taking direction some times and on one journey when he was driving Dick told him to turn left. Then a bit louder TURN LEFT NOW! Well, this did not happen and we wound up high and dry on a gravel bar. I mean you could walk around the boat in tennis shoes and not get your feet wet. As soon as we were stopped with the engine turned off our grandson asked, "What do we do now, Grandpa?" To this Dick replied, "Well you get out and help get us back into the water." Our Grandson said that it was not his fault but Grandpa's fault for letting him drive. You can imagine how that comment went over like a lead balloon with Grandpa.

Everyone got out of the boat and we all started to push and lever the boat around towards the water. This took a while as we stopped for a break now and then but thankfully the grandchildren never complained. It was a happy moment when we were floating and the engine was running once again.

Another time when our son, Jeff, was visiting during our grandchildren's stay Grandpa took the group out for an exploring trip in the boat while I was busy doing laundry and other housework. They were gone for quite a while and when I heard the boat return I went outside in time to see our grandson running for the cabin yelling, "Grandma, you won't believe what Grandpa did." Then he proceeded to tell me all about their boat trip before anyone else arrived at the cabin. When my husband and son walked up they took our grandson aside and explained to him that if you ever want to go exploring with us again you will learn to keep your mouth shut and not come back telling Grandma everything! I hugged our grandson and told him he could tell me anything and remember that Grandma is the maker of the cookies around here! This brought many laughs all around. They had been up into several different sloughs and even jumped over beaver dams with the boat. They practiced making instant turn a rounds with the boat and even got stuck one time. All of them were just having fun and playing with the biggest kid in the world, my husband!

Sometimes we have big log jams that block the main channel of water and we go out and cut them away to open the channel up. This can be quite exciting at times when you have one person driving the boat trying to hold it steady in the swirling water currents while a second person hangs over the side or back of the boat using a chain saw to cut the logs up. Dick and I have done this job many times by ourselves but on this occasion we had our son, Jeff, visiting and he wanted to help. Jeff was running the chain saw, Dick was doing the driving while I was giving directions to the driver since he is unable to see the person doing the sawing. We were having problems holding the boat steady and told Jeff to let the saw go, because the saw was jammed in a log at this point, and we had to pull away for a minute. Instead of letting the saw go Jeff hung on and was yanked right off the back of our boat. He jumped for the logs and I have never seen anyone do such a great job of walking on water, then running across floating logs to get to safety. Man could he maneuver on air! This really scared all of us because one of the biggest dangers around a log jam is getting swept under the logs and drowning. That evening back at our cabin Jeff started playing his guitar and singing a song he made up about his Dad trying to drown him in the river. The song was pretty funny and we laughed each time Jeff sang his new song. We are so lucky to have a family with a special sense of humor and to find this humor in some of the most astonishing adventures of our lives.

One summer we let our youngest son who was 17 at the time take our boat and his friend off on an Alaskan adventure of their own. They had a great time after parking the boat on the trailer at a friends and driving our truck into town. Anyway, this is not about their trip but about their return to the cabin. Jeff was so happy to be doing all the driving and launching of the boat by himself and in his hurry to get home he launched the boat and tied it to a tree on the riverbank. Then Jeff drove off to park the truck and make sure it was all locked up. When he and his friend returned to the boat they found it sitting on the bottom with about two feet of water inside. In Jeff's haste he had forgotten to put the drain plug back in and the boat sank. Now he was busy trying to pull the boat up out of the water enough to drain it before he finally figured out to use the truck to pull the boat. It was not long before the two boys had the boat drained and the plug put back in. Then they had to work on getting the outboard motor started which took a while. Thankfully Jeff had some experience with wet engines after traveling with us. This experience couldn't be ignored by us because they arrived at the cabin with a lot of wet camping gear. That drain plug was never forgotten again by any of us.

On one of the fall hunting/camping trips up the river Dick and I were exploring several sloughs and other places that we could get the boat into. Sometimes we would have to slide over a beaver dam or across a very shallow place in the water but the boat was quite strong and seemed to handle this just fine. In one spot on the main river we managed to hit a large rock that was submerged but after checking things out it looked like we did not sustain any damage. So after a few days we started home, which was eighty or ninety miles down river. Dick noticed that the boat felt a bit sluggish and he added a little more power to the throttle as we had just been taking our time and slowly moving along enjoying the scenery and wildlife. Suddenly Dick asked me to take the wheel and he went back to lift the engine cover and check the bilge. We had water coming in around the jet intake which must have been slightly bent when we struck that rock. Dick pulled over to the river bank so we could see if we could fix our problem and that was not going to happen here. So we proceeded to drive down the river with the bilge pump going continually spewing a one inch stream of water out all the way back to our cabin. Once home we were able to turn the boat around so that the stern was up on the gravel where we could jack it up and have all the tools necessary to try to stop the leak. That job took most of a day to complete but in the end we were able to continue running the boat without any problem and did not have to worry about taking on water in the bilge.

Just last summer we went to town one beautiful sunshiny day for some major shopping and on our way home we found the water level in the river had risen quite a bit. When we had to dodge pieces of logs and other floating debris we were wondering just what the famous Koepke Slough log jam would be like this evening. Well it was not long before we found out. The complete log jam near the up river end of the slough had totally moved blocking the river. We would up with three boats all stopped on the gravel bar making plans to cut the logs away some to create an opening for river traveling. Dick used our boat, with a man from Welty's family off another boat along to run our chain saw while leaning off the bow of our boat, and proceeded to cut away at logs for an opening just a bit wider than needed for passage. The third boat was an airboat, Mark and Michelle Leonard, and they were cutting logs away from a shallow area to make a passage for airboats to use. Mark could stand right out in the water to cut his logs. Before long we had a couple of routes through the log jam while the rest of us stood on the gravel bar talking. When Dick stopped his engine to clear the jets of debris from the slow idling through all the log jam work he found it would not run correctly and he made his way over to the river bank just up river from the log jam. I was given a ride up to our boat to be with Dick but after discovering our problem was not going to be fixed right away I asked the Welty's if they could drop me off at our cabin on their way by. Of course they did this as well as taking most of my groceries with me. Dick was brought home later after more mechanic work to find out the problem with our boat. This was the very first time we had left our boat tied up to the river bank so forlorn to spend the next 24 hours without any surveillance from us. The boat sat more than two miles down river from our cabin.

The next day a young man, Tim Oleson, brought up a new starter for our engine and took Dick back to our boat to get it working. Tim stayed with Dick and made sure it was going to work but that did not help as it was the wrong starter. So we were back to being without a boat again. Then another neighbor, John Binkley, called asking us what we needed and he flew out a new starter to us, landing on our gravel bar in front of the cabin where we used our canoe to meet him. Now that is some service we could never repay!! Anyway, the new starter did the trick and we were back in business again with an operating boat. We even had the old starter rebuilt and keep a spare right at our cabin now as John suggested.

In 1996 we bought a small 36 foot sailboat in Gig Harbor, Washington. Then we took a week long sailing course in Bellingham, Washington before heading out on a five year circumnavigation of the world. That is a complete book in itself, OUR JOURNALS OF SAILING THE WORLD ON S/V MERMAID, but the reason for bringing it up here is that after five years of not running the river here at home we saw many big changes on our first summer back at home. Dick is still so good at reading the river that we only made a two wrong turns where new channels had been made in our absence but one could not see them in advance. We felt pretty good about our trip home after all those years. It seems that experience really pays off as we seem to go many years without any major boating problems now. But one must always be ready for the odd mechanical problems that occur when traveling in the wilderness. We have seen a few problems ourselves.

Chapter 17

BUILDING AN AIRPLANE

In the late 1980's we had decided to build our own aircraft and to do this we needed to have a workshop. So the first thing we had to do was to start making the lumber needed using our small chain saw mill and setting that lumber aside to dry. One winter we spent most weekends falling trees and cutting lumber then stacking it with spacers between the pieces to allow the air to circulate and dry the wood until we had enough to start on the shop. By the summer of 1986 we had a good clearing made for the shop, all the twenty five holes dug for the foundation poles, and several logs pealed and ready to build walls. After the flood of August 1986 and the time to clean up the mess in our yard we started our new construction project. Since Dick was working full time we only worked on the building during weekends in the summer and fall. By the summer of 1988 we had the shop building up with a roof on it. The next thing was to cut in the doors and window spaces.

Our oldest son, Robert, and his family had driven to Alaska for a summer vacation and to spend a week or so with us. This worked great as Robert helped his Dad make a four foot wide shop door and they covered the window holes with two layers of clear plastic sheeting to keep the bugs out. Robert and Tina proceeded to sleep in the shop during their stay. We kept the two grandchildren in the cabin with us. It was fun to have them with us even though just a short time. After this visit from them we established a routine of flying the grandchildren up for a summer vacation with us every other year. I will write more about this later..

In 1989 Dick and I decided to make one small corner of the shop into a bathroom with a bathtub/shower, vanity sink and "honey bucket" toilet. We were just working on putting in another driven point well for the shop when we had a visitor from California, John

Norris. He wanted to help us so we three finished driving that well and putting the tub into the bathroom. We always enjoyed having John visit as he was like one of our sons and had grown up around our boys.

Just outside the bathroom we put in a shelf for the well pitcher pump and a small two burner propane hotplate. The hotplate was used to make tea when working out in the shop. Then we installed a double laundry sinks along one wall where I could use my wringer washer with ease. Dick and I hand dug another cesspool (8x8x8 feet) and lined it with logs for our sink and tub drains to go into. Now we felt very modern indeed because we had a lovely shower room and laundry facilities in a heated building. We even built a set of bunks for overflow guests to sleep in the shop.

The biggest problem was that during the winter months you had to plan ahead and get the fires going a day in advance when one wanted to shower or do laundry. We did not keep the shop warm except for when it was to be used. This saved immensely on firewood consumption.

The shop turned out to be 24x24 feet inside with a high work bench running along one wall for 24 feet with three windows along the work bench for light. Dick was finally able to have his tools in one place and to mount a vise, grinder and other tools on his bench. We had purchased a rolling tool box with multiple drawers that held all the smaller loose tools and hand held power tools. Before we could start to build an airplane we had to purchase a few major power tools to complete our shop. Within a year we had installed a floor standing drill press, band saw, table saw, air compressor and welder. Dick loved his shop now and was ready to take on a major project.

We had a covered 8x24 foot porch on both the front and rear of the shop with 4 foot wide ramps leading up to them. The rear porch was our snow machine garage, keeping our machines under cover and out of the sun while high enough to avoid flood waters. The front porch wound up being our airplane hangar after a couple of years.

In 1991 we ordered a complete kit for building a KIT FOX

airplane which is a two seat, side by side, tail dragger. We were amazed when the crate was delivered to Fairbanks and could hardly wait to get the huge crate up the river. We wound up unloading the crate and putting the pieces right into our boat because the crate was far to large for us to move. Once we had the boat up the river we then started to unload all the items and put them in our shop. This was fun and exciting for us. The next job was finally started as we unpack the various small boxes and inventory all the pieces, we were shocked at how much goes into one small plane. This was going to be a BIG PROJECT! Over the next two years we worked on the construction of the airplane together as often as we could manage. It was not long before we learned to hate the word FABRICATE because it meant that particular job would take a few days to complete as we made parts. We kept a running diary about our work days which is fun to look back on with all the details of the plane construction. It took us more than a thousand working hours to build the plane and most of that time we were working together. We took a lot of photos as we were building so we would have a nice scrap book to go with our diary.

The first time we took the plane out of our shop to sit in our front yard so we could install the wings was a mighty big day. On this day we took a special photo for our annual Christmas card to share with all our friends and family. We are very proud of this accomplishment. Many people start to build an airplane but few of them are completed. This project took us two years to complete so we are now into 1993. We are getting excited about the test flight of our airplane.

As you already know we live about 30 miles up the Salcha River where there are no roads. So the airplane had to be moved into Fairbanks to get the FAA inspection and release for the test flight. Our youngest son, Jeff, came up the river to help us take the airplane into town. Jeff did not want to miss out on the fun. This was quite an interesting feat in itself. First we had to take the top rack and cover off our boat so we had a much larger area to put the airplane. Using ¾ inch plywood we made a solid deck across the back seats for the airplane to rest on with the tail wheel sitting on more plywood out over the swim platform of the boat. Then we tied our boat out from the bank with the bow facing the middle of the river, which is very hard to keep the boat from moving in the current. Next we put our ramps down to the boat from the top of the river bank. Now we were ready to move the airplane out of our yard. The KITFOX wings fold back against the fuselage and lock into place giving us a narrower profile to go between all the tall spruce trees. Dick, Jeff and I managed to get the airplane onto the boat and tied down securely for a 30 mile boat ride to the highway. Now this was quite a sight to see, we had the only aircraft carrier on the river that day! There were other times when planes that have crashed far up river were carried down on boats in pieces but ours was new and quite flyable. The big concern at this point was can we get the boat on step so it will flow down the river correctly. The only way to answer this is just get out and try to do it. So after closing up the cabin and shop that is just what the three of us did. Once we were in motion and motoring smoothly we started laughing at the sight of our aircraft carrier. This was really fun and many of the neighbors down river heard about us coming down with the airplane, so they were out on the river bank taking photos of us.

The next thing we knew we were at the highway and loading our boat onto the trailer with the airplane riding piggy back on the boat. Now we did not check with the state troopers to see if it was legal to haul this type of load on the highway but just assumed that since we were not over-wide we were alright. We had telephoned the FAA and the Fairbanks International Airport Security to get permission to launch our boat at the airport float pond so we could off load the airplane easier. Once the boat was launched in the pond Dick backed the boat up to the launch ramp and we tied it to our truck on one side and a sign post on the other side to hold it in place. Then it was just a matter of reversing the loading process using the same ramps. This was very exciting as we hoped to have it all go off without any problems and not drop our plane into the water. That would be a disaster. We had a couple of airport security vehicles come over just to watch the unusual scene. As soon as the airplane was on solid ground Dick started the engine and taxied over to the transient parking while Jeff and I followed with the boat back on the boat trailer. It was such a wonderful sight to see our little blue airplane sitting at the International Airport. The next thing we did was to use the airport's compass rose and complete our compass correction card. Now we are ready to fly.

We were scheduled for the FAA airworthiness check four days later and could hardly wait to find out if our airplane was cleared to fly. We were cleared on the very first FAA check and Dick was told that he
must put on about 25 hours right around the local flying area before he could fly the airplane home or take passengers with him. So now we are to the point of the first test flight.

Two days after our certification Dick and I went to the airport for him to test fly our very own hand built airplane. Our friend, Ruth, drove out with her video camera to record for history all of this. Dick was so happy that I thought his face would split. All you could see was teeth in the smile. I had a hand held aircraft radio so I could follow his progress from the transient parking area. Dick taxied to the end of the general aviation runway and proceeded to do two very high speed taxis down the runway to get the feel of the aircraft controls. First he would lift one wing just enough to clear the main landing gear from the tarmac, he would then repeat the process with the other wing. Now Ruth and I heard Dick ask the tower for permission to take off. I was so nervous I thought I would wet my pants! My stomach was in my chest as I watched my husband lift off and fly away over the Tanana Flats. I cried from excitement and pride in him as I danced around the parking area! Then I began to watch him do various maneuvers like stalls, steep turns and such to check out each aspect of the flight characteristics. I was becoming more relaxed as I watched Dick fly then he came in and requested permission for doing some "touch and go" landings. That first landing was absolutely perfect but I was holding my breath. Then I was able to finally relax and enjoy his flight. When he landed for the last time that day and taxied into the parking area his face was almost frozen into a huge grin. I think Dick was a bit overwhelmed as well because he never even tried to get out of the airplane immediately, possibly his legs were weak right then! When he stopped and turned the engine off he was rattling on so fast talking about the flight that we had to slow him down some to understand. This was a day and one flight that Dick will remember forever.

As soon as Dick had enough hours to get cleared from the local area for flight he started flying the KITFOX to and from our cabin to work. This worked out so very well and was a great deal more economical than our Cessna 170 was to fly. After building the KITFOX we hardly ever used the Cessna 170 and eventually we sold the old Cessna after owning and flying it for more than 26 years.

We had put together skis for our little plane for the coming winter months and as soon as the river froze and the snow was on the ground we had a great time out exploring our world. The whole world opened up with this tiny airplane because we could get it into some very tight places with ease. We would find any excuse to go for a flight, even just a few miles up river to a neighbor's house for coffee and a visit. To say this plane was fun is putting it very mildly.

Eventually it became my turn to learn to fly the KITFOX. Dick would ride in the right hand seat and I would practice various maneuvers until I became confident with the plane. We would often fly down to the lodge on the highway to have lunch or breakfast and pick up our mail. This was a fun outing for us. On one particular winter day I was the pilot and we were landing on a small strip next door to the lodge. When I approached the field I could see where someone had left zig-zagging snow machine tracks on the runway. I really was not concerned but thought I needed to stay aware because those tracks can throw you around a bit. When I hit the first snow machine track it veered the plane to one side abruptly and I gave the correct rudder a push but nothing happened. Before we knew it I was off into the willow bushes fully stopped and grumbling about that stupid error. Dick asked me why I had not given it full rudder and I replied that I had pushed the rudder all the way. Then Dick got out of the airplane and came around to the pilot's doorway. Dick asked me to give it full rudder and then he pushed the pedal another couple of inches. Dick was laughing so hard but I finally managed to understand him, "You gave it full KayD leg but the rudder had more movement! You need to fly with a pillow behind your back and butt so your feet reach the pedals better." Well, I didn't think this was so funny and my pride was hurt because I screwed up my landing. Thankfully nothing else was hurt. Then Dick said, "Oh well Honey, you are now a genuine bush pilot as here we sit in the bushes!" It is amazing that he did not get smacked for that comment. Then when we went into the lodge for our mail Dick had to tell my bush flying story to everyone which brought great laughter all around. I now have a thick sturdy cushion that goes behind when I am pilot. Our seats are stationary in the KITFOX.

We both love to fly with the plane on skis as you can land almost anywhere in Alaska during the winter. It really opens up the country. The smoothness of the landings and the long runway stretches makes it so nice. Dick has taken many people up for rides just to have some fun exploring. One day when I was pilot again Dick talked me into landing in a small meadow area on a frozen pond. The landing was going well but we didn't seem to be slowing down enough for me and Dick said to just wait, I would stop before the trees on the other side. Sure enough we stopped and I turned the plane around immediately ready for take off in the opposite direction. It was a very calm day and we were having fun learning the limits of our aircraft. After several different landings we headed back home. This is sort of like going out four wheeling but using an airplane instead.

One thing about doing bush flying like that, it is almost certain that one day you have a mishap that requires a bit of airplane repair work. We have had our share of minor dings and such. That is when you bring the airplane back to our shop and fix whatever needs repaired so we can continue to go out having fun. Dick is also the certified mechanic for our plane so we can legally do all our own repairs.

In the summer months we usually land on the highway out in front of the lodge and then taxi into their parking lot. This is quite easy as one can see a long way down the road to check for traffic before committing to land. Several times we have had to fly around in circles waiting for the traffic to clear. Sometimes this can cause a stir of excitement when they have customers that have never seen an airplane land on the roadway. Many times we have had tourist come along and take a photo of us fueling our airplane at the gas pumps in front of the lodge. Then we always have a fun conversation with some new people. The nice part is landing on a road in Alaska is perfectly fine as long as you do not interrupt traffic. When we would do this down in California to visit friends who lived in the country the state Highway Patrol frowned on it. We were told to keep off the roads so we had to resort to fields and dirt trails down there.

Chapter 18

BUSH FLYING ADVENTURES

When you have your own airplane in Alaska it really opens the country to you. Alaska is one fifth the size of the contiguous 48 United States and has very few roads outside of the cities. Most of the country is only accessible by aircraft. I believe that Alaska has the most licensed pilots than any other state and the most privately owed aircraft per capita. Dick and I have always loved having a good tail-dragger, the third wheel is on the tail instead of the nose of the craft, making bush flying much easier. One can fly for many hours in the wilderness without seeing towns or civilization as you cross mountain ranges, rivers and tundra areas. Wildlife viewing from the air is fabulous and you don't even frighten the animals. Sometimes a large moose will stop feeding and look around then go right back to feeding or resting. We have been able to view magnificent swans in small lakes, on their nests, which was unforgettable, as well as many other water fowl without doing any harm to the flora or fauna.

This state is so very beautiful and has so much to offer in the way of outdoor activities. We enjoy visiting remote villages and getting to know better the native cultures. It seems that each area of the state has very unique topography, native skills and arts. One can spend a life time learning from the many people of Alaska.

As you are flying in the bush most often without maintained runways, landing on gravel bars, beaches, frozen lakes, hill tops or wherever to get close to your destination, you will most likely have a few mishaps or incidents with your airplane. We have been very fortunate to have had only a few incidents which were easily fixed by ourselves.

On our home strip, a gravel bar on a bend in the river across from our cabin, the water was often too high leaving a minimum landing area so we would proceed to land on the water and roll up onto the gravel bar which increased our landing site by quite a bit. This worked out very well for us over the many years we have lived here. But there were times when we had to move our plane off the runway in a hurry as the flood waters were taking over the gravel bar. Then we left the plane in town or at the lodge on the highway and used our boat to commute until the water receded, usually not more than a couple of days. After this happened we had to walk the runway/gravel bar throwing all the sticks, large rocks and debris off the landing site.

One year after a big flood we found a huge eight foot high log jam deposited right across the middle of our runway which took us a few days to cut apart and remove so we could use the landing site again. The high water always left some cuts and dips in the runway which we had to fill in with gravel and smooth out the surface. This was done the old fashioned way using a shovel, rake and wheel barrow. Great exercise! In 1993 we purchased a Polaris six wheeler with a dump bed on the rear along with a plow blade for the front end and a drag box/blade for the rear. This machine made the runway upkeep so much easier as we could move more gravel and smooth the dips in a lot less time. We would have to load the 6-wheeler onto our boat and transport it across the river to the runway, spend the time needed to fix up the runway and drag it, then repeat the loading and transporting the machine back to our home property. This usually took us a full day and sometimes two days if the water damage was excessive to the runway. Each year in the spring we take a push mower across the river to mow the brush down about forty feet wide and the length of the runway. Also, every few years we have to trim back some of the tree branches that grow out too far into our runway area, using a small chain saw. As you can see it does take a lot of work to maintain a runway in the bush.

One must always be aware of the weather too so we can get our plane off the runway during flood stages. Listening to the weather reports daily is very important because it is not always what is happening at home but more than 100 miles up the river in a heavy rain storm. We have figured out that it takes about 12 hours for any flood waters way up the river to reach our home runway so we have sufficient time to move any gear that may be damaged from a flood.

During the winter months we have a catalytic propane heater that we place inside our engine cowling to heat the engine before take off. When Dick was commuting to town for work every day we put the engine heater on low when we went to bed so it was warm by morning. The wings were always covered and the engine cowl had an insulated quilt that wrapped around it to help hold the heat in. Often we had to run a rope along the fuselage and tail sections to remove any frost before take off. These were some of the differences in pre-flight of the plane compared to living in warmer climates.

Also during the winter months we went to bed earlier so that we could arise at 4am in case the weather conditions indicated a "no fly" day. The stopping weather conditions were temperatures colder than 30 below zero Fahrenheit and/or having very low visibility from fog or snow. At those times Dick would turn off the aircraft engine heater first thing in the morning and proceed into town by snow machine 30 miles to the highway then by car another 44 miles making it a two hour commute. Many people thought this was quite a bother but it didn't seem so to us, because the beautiful peace and quiet of life on the river was more than worth the extra effort. We just changed our time at home together to the mornings instead of the evenings where we chat, read or whatever we want to do. This worked well over the many years before Dick retired in 1994.

Often in the winter time we would decide to just go take an airplane ride for fun and to visit friends at their cabins. This was always great fun and we would take turns being the pilot in command which kept me up on my skills too. Landing on skis instead of wheels can be a challenge at times because you do not have any brakes. One time we landed about 30 miles up the river from our home to visit some neighbors and the ice was quite slick when I touched down for landing so we proceeded to slide right on by their cabin and had to turn around and come back under power to park on the river in front of their cabin. They asked if we were just teasing them by sliding on by which made us laugh!

Dick has always enjoyed taking anyone for a flight just to get out and play in the air. Exploring the many mining areas, valleys and lakes while the ground is frozen is quite an adventure. Often we park the plane and hike further in towards an interesting spot to explore. We cannot even remember some of the people we have taken flying to many places around this state of Alaska, some even visitors from foreign countries who were very impressed with the immenseness of the country.

Many times we would fly down to the highway and land on the road before taxiing up to the lodge to refuel at the gas pumps, our plane used regular auto gas, and would pick up our mail. This was always a good excuse to have lunch or breakfast out at the lodge too. It was not a surprise to most of the local people for us to land for coffee or a visit, but quite a shock for visitors to our state. Then it was fun to share our adventures and have a chat with the newcomers before flying off into the blue skies and home.

We have had the wonderful opportunity to share our lifestyle with many visitors from all over the world by taking them home with us for a day or more, sometimes up to a week, to see what living in a remote log cabin is like. I think the most often heard comment from them is, "Wow, this is so beautiful, quiet and peaceful but much more work daily than we expected!" This brings a laugh from us as we realize that our life is not meant for the weak or lazy. On the other hand, we tell people that anyone can do this if they have the will. We are not rich people, never have been, and we have learned everything we do by reading and good old hard work. Many times we mess things up and have to do it over but then that is education and education costs money and time. We usually do not make the same mistakes again and in the meantime we have certainly learned a lot of different things. Our motto is "it is a bad day if you haven't learned something new."

On one flight we landed on a gravel bar with a light tailwind because there was no other choice and we nicked our propeller during the roll out. Dick proceeded to take the propeller off and we slowly hammered out the two ends to make them flat again so we could get airborne and back to town to purchase a new propeller. That worked out just fine and we had a new propeller the next day.

We are firm believers that any flight you walk away from and the damage to the plane is minimal is a good flight when flying in the bush. If a person flies off bush lands very much it is not uncommon for minor mishaps now and then. Sometimes it is as simple as putting a small stick into a tire causing a flat or breaking a tail wheel spring. Although we are happy to say we have had very few minor incidents, the worst case being in the very first year we owned our first airplane which I described in part one of this book.

We had so many hours of fun family time in our old 1950 Cessna 170-A for more than 300,000 miles over 26 years. Our sons and many of their friends spent a good deal of time in that plane with us. We have so many grand memories for all the family flying to off road areas.

Living in Alaska makes you feel like you are in another country altogether because it is so far away from the rest of the USA. When Alaskans travel to the lower 48 states they are "taking a trip outside" which is quite an expensive and big under taking. From Fairbanks it is about 2500 miles to the state of Washington by road. That is almost like traveling from the east coast to the west coast of the United States. We can fly that distance in our airplane with only two overnight stops and can carry a lot of baggage (camping and survival gear included). Since 1977 we have made so many round trips in our plane we quit counting them. These trips can vary in time but the route stays pretty much the same as we like to travel the trench in Canada from Watson Lake to Prince George. Flying the Alaska Highway route is not as nice because of all the traffic, towns and people. The scenery and remoteness is so awesome.

In years past the route through the trench in Canada was very desolate but has since become more populated with timber and mining camps, roads and small villages. One use to fly for

500 miles or more without seeing civilization. Often the weather reports were wrong for the trench area and we would get caught in some terrible thunderstorms or even snow white out conditions. We knew exactly how high the surrounding mountains were and always kept exact position of our aircraft along the way. This was mostly pilot-age and dead reckoning flying. There were two small dirt landing strips in the trench for native villages. One time we landed at one to purchase more fuel, because of the winds we were running a bit short on fuel to make our destination. Thankfully we were able to purchase some at a very high price though.

One of our flights heading north in the trench turned into a real stressful situation. It was winter time and we had been given a good weather forecast with some clouds between Prince George, BC and Watson Lake, Yukon. We had been flying along quite nicely and had past the point of no return, not enough fuel to go back, some time back when a snow storm hit with a vengeance. Since our destination was clear Dick climbed up and out over the snow storm but for a few minutes it was a very uncomfortable feeling not being able to see anything out the windows. Eventually we were on top and made a good flight to our destination at Watson Lake. The time passing as we flew over the cloud cover and still could not see the ground makes a person start to worry about finding the airport of destination. Thankfully both of us had plenty of flight time learning to use dead reckoning that we manage to do quite well without getting upset. The trench was famous for throwing a curve ball into a flight and you had to be ready for whatever happened. Eventually the clouds broke and we were exactly where we were suppose to be and could see the airport in the distance. It was just another beautiful and safe landing.

On another flight through the trench Dick picked up some strong winds from the tail making him arrive about 1 hour sooner in Watson Lake than expected. Wow the fuel mileage was great on that trip! More often the strong winds through there were just bumpy and rough making the flight seem like forever.

One year we were headed out of state to visit family and friends. The weather suddenly turned very nasty on our way south from

Whitehorse to Watson Lake, Yukon. We had just passed over Rancheria River Lodge along the Alaska Highway when we found ourselves in real whiteout conditions. There was no way we could continue on to Watson Lake with all the hills around so we made a quick turn around 180 degrees and back tracked to the Rancheria Lodge where we proceeded to land on the highway and taxi in to park in their parking lot using an old truck for a tie down. The truck was buried in the snow so we figured it was not going anywhere. When we went into the lodge to find a telephone to call the Canadian air traffic controllers the people in there asked where we came from. After explaining the white out conditions in the air they seemed surprised we were able to land at all. Even the air traffic control asked how we landed there due to the curves in the highway with mountains on both sides. It was just nice to be on the ground safe and warm! So we took a room at the lodge until morning and it was not long before we were joined by several truck drivers that parked for the night as well. Everyone was amazed that we had been flying that day. That was probably one of the worst weather conditions we ever encountered.

In 1993 or 94 Dick left our cabin for a couple of days to go hunting about 100 miles or more upriver from our home. He was well equipped with camping gear, food and other supplies and very anxious to fly our new KITFOX IV off on a fun trip. He found a great place to land the plane and had a good time but no luck getting any wild game meat. Dick came home excited and wanted to take me out to see some of the area he had seen.

A few days later we went flying and I was surprised to see how very many mining sites there are around here. I guess at one time many years ago our river was involved in the gold rush. We knew a couple of miners that worked two claims back in the 1970-80's and had visited their sites during that time. During some of our flight time Dick found a neat clearing on top of a mountain but decided not to land there because we had not even told anyone that we were going off flying or when to expect us home again. These were precautions we always took as a safety measure by telling a friend or neighbor of our flight plans. Luckily we never had to utilize a rescue for ourselves but have known of people that were searched for. Some make it back alright and others do not.

Our youngest son was always very interested in flying and would go out with his Dad anytime to just play and practice maneuvers. Quite often when Jeff was visiting us I could hear them in the air off to the side of our place out over the tundra practicing stalls and such. I am sure if I could hear the conversations in the plane they would be laughing and having great fun together. When the two of them landed you could hardly see for the glare off their teeth in the sunshine because of huge smiles!

Chapter 19

SOCIALIZING

We are often asked just what we do for socializing living way out in the country without road access. First of all when you live out like that you are very busy with just your daily living chores such as cutting, hauling, splitting and stacking firewood, which we use about ten cord of wood per year for the heat stove and our cook stove combined. Before we had a well we had to haul our water from the river and boil all the drinking water to prevent getting any illnesses. Our lighting was all kerosene lamps which had to be filled daily (twice a day on the short winter days) and cleaning the chimneys often. I have ground wheat for my own flour for baking more than 45 years now along with baking all our bread, cookies and other goodies. So you can see all of this takes a bit of time each day. Then in the summers we have a small garden to tend, fish to catch, hunting season to get our moose and caribou then canning and freezer wrapping to do. Fall finds berry picking in full swing and making jams, syrups and juices. In other words it is like living back in the old days where one is busy taking care of themselves and their needs.

Summers are filled with building projects, gathering foods and hunting mostly. We do take time to have a few "get together" with friends over the various holidays (Memorial Day, Fourth of July and Labor Day weekends) where we barbecue, play volleyball and visit. Often we have friends and/or neighbors come by for visits and lunch or dinner with us. Many times we will have visitors from the lower 48 states during this time as well. We have enjoyed many visitors from foreign countries over the years which add a bit of fun for us.

Most of our socializing is done in the winters when the snow is on the ground and life slows to a nice pace with more freedom to play. We do use snow machines, motorized tracked vehicles that look much like a motorcycle, to travel among our neighbors and have tea or coffee, sometimes many miles away. Often times we have a fun dinner or lunch with a few couples. We have had holiday cookie exchange parties, white elephant parties to get rid of our junk, and just any old excuse to party with our friends and neighbors. We love to work jig saw puzzles in the winter, do crossword puzzles and Sudoku puzzles. When we had children at home or visiting we play board games, dominoes and card games.

Another great pastime is music. We have an old player piano that we completely rebuilt in 1970 with about 400 piano rolls that we love to sit and play while singing along. Many of our family members play musical instruments (violin, guitar, accordion, harmonica, percussion) and we love to have some fun together with them.

Dick is always busy working on some project or another as he enjoys constructing things. He loves his great workshop. I enjoy knitting, sewing and other projects which keep me busy with all the family to knit for. It was a great pleasure to make quilts for our grandchildren. My favorite past time is to read almost anything I can get my hands on, especially non-fiction and biographical.

Since we retired we stay at home more and only go into town once a month for groceries or other needs. That means our trips are well planned so we can shop at the grocery, pharmacy, hardware, auto parts, building supply, fuel depot and any other places necessary. Then we meet friends in town for lunch together at various places. These are full days as we leave home at 7am and usually do not get back until 7pm or later. Summer time we take the boat down the river about 30 miles to the highway where we then take our vehicle another 44 miles into town. Winter time we travel by snow machine to the highway, then vehicle to town. The commute takes about two hours one way and two hours back. Then we have to be sure we have all our supplies packed for transportation in the boat or snow machine sled that we pull. After we get home it is the same normal process that you would have to unload everything and put it all away. To say the least, our shopping excursions are a real full day and get quite exhausting. The following day is usually a day sort of resting except for what must be done. We use ice chests at all times during the year because we pack them with perishables and warm water bottles in the winter to avoid freezing. Many times I just wrap produce in newspaper and pack it in a cardboard box and put the box into my insulated bag on the back of my snow machine, this will keep produce from freezing for a couple of hours even at 40 below zero temperatures outdoors.

Every day we try to take a nice walk through the woods and/or out on the frozen river checking out the various animal tracks and enjoying the beauty of the country. Most of the time on our walks we stay within a mile or so of home but sometimes we go as far as three miles or more in one direction. Then when we are really tired after a hard day of work we will sit out in our wood fired hot tub on the deck and watch the birds and world go by for relaxation. It is not always work, work, work around here!

One of the nice things about living like this is that everyone really knows each other and will do anything to help each other. Often times we get together to help someone move their cabin back from the eroding river bank, or haul ice in March to fill everyone's ice house for the summer months. One time we had a group here to help us raise a 60 foot huge HAM radio antenna in our back yard. Some people even get into the roofing of a new building not belonging to them. Life is filled with good works from friends and neighbors helping each other.

If anyone is experiencing a major health problem you can bet on your friends and neighbors coming to visit or lend a helping hand with chores. We have been at both ends of this spectrum and really appreciate everyone more than words can say.

These are the things that make life so good plus the satisfaction of knowing that we do most everything ourselves so we see a beginning and completion of all projects right here at home. I wish our younger generation could feel that goodness at times to know they DID IT THEMSELVES. There is not much we would not attempt to try by ourselves even if we had to purchase a book to find out how to do it. We are firm believers that if one can read a book one can accomplish anything in life.

As the years progress we have seen many neighbors move into town for health reasons or due to ageing and we miss them all dearly. So when we can we try to meet them in town for lunch and a good chat now and then. Many of the older folks have died but we still think of them often and the many fun times we shared in the past. The cycles of life are always changing but it is never dull when you live away from the normal flow of people.

Now we have the next younger generation growing up, buying land, building cabins, having babies and looking after the older folks on the river. When we have parties we have multi-generations attending and everyone having fun together. Most parties are what we call "pot luck" and everyone brings some food to share and all their own drinks. Sometimes we have huge bonfires or even fireworks in the winter time with quite a group of folks enjoying it altogether.

Chapter 20

FAMILY LIFE IN THE BUSH

So many people we meet ask us what it is like to raise a family so far out of town and touch with society. Actually it was not hard for us as we have lived out like this since our first child was born. It was great to have two boys because they could play together and have their own adventures. Both our sons have learned to do most anything from construction, fishing, hunting, cooking, laundry to whatever is necessary to maintain a normal lifestyle in the bush. They grew up off the "grid" where we furnished our own water, power and sewer systems. So it was not new for them to remember to turn off unnecessary lights, take quick showers or baths and to entertain themselves since we did not have television until their late teen years. I guess you can say they grew up being "green" with the waste not want not attitude of today's new culture. We were not perfect parents but we did our best to give them a good life and get them ready to take care of themselves as adults. Like every family we had some rough times too but we are very proud of our sons and now their families too.

Dick and I have always liked music so our home had instruments around from the beginning. We purchased and completely rebuilt an old 1930 player piano in 1970 which took us about 90 hours to finish. All the bellows, about 105, had to be taken apart and rebuilt with new leather and valves to make each key play and so much more. This was quite a huge project, but fun for us to work on each evening and on weekends until we had it playing like new again. We found the QRS Player Piano Company where we purchased a catalog and could order parts, materials and even piano rolls to play. Then we started a grand collection of about 400 piano rolls, covering classical, country, old-time sing-a-long songs, musical shows, and many children's songs. The boys loved to sit and play the piano rolls by pumping the pedals making the machine work. Singing using the words printed on each roll increased their reading ability and helped them learn about American History at the same time. Our grandchildren have also enjoyed many hours at the same piano. Now we are ready for our great-grandchildren to have the same fun in life.

Besides for the above mentioned piano we have an accordion, violin, guitar, complete set of harmonicas and several percussion instruments. It was always fun to sit and make some music together with a lot of singing and laughing. Our youngest son could play various string instruments quite well and went on to play in the school orchestras for seven years and county wide honor orchestra for three years. Our oldest son played accordion for a short time and loved drumming. We always felt that a family who plays together stays together and has a great time. I know we sure did.

We are all avid readers and I would read aloud to us in the evenings after the work was done and whenever we were on long auto trips. Making reading fun and enjoyable we never made our sons read but furnished them with books and magazines of things that interested them, such as National Wildlife, National Geographic, westerns, wilderness adventures and interesting biographies. Everyone went to bed early as we were always up early each day to commute to town or go play somewhere.

In the winter time we would snow shoe hike, ice skate on the frozen river, put together jig saw puzzles, play board games and do handcrafts. The boys made many gifts for their grandmothers over the years and for Dad and Mom. We still have many of them and cherish the thought and time put into the making of the gifts. The boys would collect obsidian and using a pointed rod chip the pieces to make arrowheads. I still have some jewelry made this way. We learned to make other jewelry (southwest Indian designs) by using colorful beads and safety pins. These are some of the ways we used our evenings together.

When you live out away from civilization and furnish all your own utilities it takes up a bit of time and work to do this daily. As I have mentioned before we spent a lot of time cutting trees and splitting wood for heat, maintaining a water supply, maintaining all the machinery we use, grinding our wheat for flour and baking all our products from scratch along with all the normal things you do each day to keep your life running. It sounds like we were working most of the time but that was not true either because we always took time out to play, even to going away one weekend a month on a camping trip somewhere. Often it was close to home back-packing and hiking or later on going to a lovely isolated desert oasis hot springs to camp and socialize with many friends there.

We have really missed not seeing our sons as often as I would like as they grew up and moved off with their lives and families. Still we have managed to get together once or twice each year and these times are very precious to us. When our sons had small children we were able to spend some fun times on unusual outings with them. Like going to a circus, camping, visiting the Pacific Science Center, theaters, state fairs, amusement parks, out for special dinners and riding on the Lady Washington sailing vessel and so much more.

In the later years the most important times were the weeks we had during the summers with our grandchildren visiting us here on the Salcha River in Alaska. Our grandchildren had the opportunity to learn to drive riverboats, fly our airplane, shoot guns properly, shoot with bows and arrows, fish and clean their catch, make many handcrafts to take home to their parents, cut trees, peel logs for a house and so much more. There were many hours spent at the piano singing or the dining table playing games. The yard was set up with a badminton court and a horseshoe pit where we played short tournaments each day. The grandchildren learned how to live off the grid and be totally self reliant along the way. We are still working on the shutting of the lights when not in use and careful use of water by turning off the faucet when brushing ones teeth but hey, Rome wasn't built in a day either! We only had a few weeks a year to teach these habits to the grandchildren, otherwise they spent their lives in the big city.

One of the toughest things to get use to was not having our children around much as adults due to our living so far away from everything and they had to work for a living. When your sons marry you sort of take a back seat as their spouses lead them in another direction, as life was meant to be I guess. But we are very lucky to have wonderful daughters-in-law that share in our sons lives in such a good manner. All of this just makes our times with family all the more enjoyable and we look forward to each visit together. Over the years we have spent many lovely holidays together, but not enough for me as I would like to have all holidays together. When one can look at the men we raised and feel pride in their lives and what they give back to the community that is what really counts. We could not have asked for more.

The memories of our grand-children sitting at the player piano singing songs together for hours at a time when it was rainy or too hot to be outdoors, even when they played the same song over and over and over! It is so cute to watch little ones reading all the words and trying hard to keep up with the music. We had many laughs over this as we sang along with them. Of course we knew many songs that the children did not know and we would burst into song about something that happened or they were doing. Finally one day they asked us, "Do you have a song for everything that goes on in life?" Dick and I answered at the same time YES!! Then we all laughed loud and long.

It was very hard to be mad or keep a sad face for long in our family! When one was feeling sorry for themselves Dick or I would shout out, "Come on now three aahs for _____." Then you would hear everyone else sing out AAH, AAH, AAH and by this time the pouting one was laughing. This always seemed to work. Yet we were always ready with a hug when they wanted one or needed one. It was hard for me to get use to more grown up children that did not want to be hugged because I am a big hugger. Then everyone grew into adults and we are back to hugging which I really like.

The question most asked from people we meet is, what happens when you have a medical emergency since we are two hours from town. Now that is a good question but then we ask them just what constitutes a real emergency? We feel that a dire emergency is something like a heart attack, stroke or broken back. Anything else is just a normal emergency and can be handled mostly right at home. We have sure had our share of those too. When our boys were growing up I would try to fix their problems with soap, water, peroxide and a bandage.

We only had two times that a doctor visit was required for a son's medical emergency. Once after the boys had been wrestling in their bedroom and Robert hit the back of his head on the corner of the dresser. He couldn't get the bleeding to stop and finally told us he needed help. When I cleaned him up and got the bleeding stopped it would start all over again as soon as he moved his head. The area would not hold a butterfly bandage when his head moved around so we took him to town for five stitches to close the wound. The next week we removed those stitches right at home. The other emergency in town was for Robert again as he had cut off the end of his left middle finger. This happened in a woodshop at school and Dick went to the hospital to take care of that since he was closer at the time. The finger was stitched back together and remained useful even if numb on the end.

Our other son, Jeff, had his share of mishaps but never had to go to emergency for repairs. When Jeff was about three he was running and pushing a large metal truck across the floor when he fell on the truck cutting his face open between the upper lip and his nose. I could see his teeth through the cut as the skin sagged. After cleaning him up and applying a couple of butterfly bandages he held an ice pack to his mouth for a while to lower the swelling. Jeff kept mumbling something so I finally removed the ice pack to understand him as he quietly said, "Mom, my mouth hurts." What an understatement that was! Jeff was also the son who came in with an arrow sticking out of his arm one day. That was also taken care of with soap, water and peroxide. We always called peroxide "bubblies" as that is what it would do when applied to a cut. Our sons would automatically get the bottle of peroxide to clean out a wound whenever they had a puncture or small cut, even skinned knees. We never had trouble with infections of wounds around our home.

When the boys were very young like before school age we had a few odd mishaps like the time Jeff was breathing so of oddly and when I checked his nose he had pushed a Pinon pine nut in the shell up his nose until it was stuck in the sinus cavity. I had a terrible time getting that nut dislodged from his nose and he never put anything in his nose again, thank heaven.

Another unusual mishap was when Robert climbed up into the back of our pickup truck to get into some trash because he could smell oranges which he really loved. In a bag he found a few oranges and ate all of them, these had been thrown away because they were molded or really bad from a crate we had been given from neighbors. It was not long before he came inside and said he did not feel good. Robert broke out with a terrible case of hives all over his body so I had him soak in a tub of baking soda water to help relive the itches. That fellow never ate anything again without asking if it was alright!!

Many times we have thanked our lucky stars to have had such a healthy family with only minor cold now and then. When any of us had an upset stomach, it usually only lasted for one day. But we did have a rule that anyone sick enough to be home was going to stay in bed which I think really helped to solve the many childish excuses for not feeling well.

One year we all came down with a bad pneumonia which was going all around town. When we went to the doctor to see if we needed help he wanted to hospitalize both Dick and Jeff but the hospital was so full they had patients in the hallways. He gave us some cough medicine, antibiotics and sent us home to care for ourselves. We wound up in our sleeping bags on the living room floor right in front of our wood fireplace so it was easy to keep putting logs on the fire to stay warm. This was the worst illness we ever had and we were all four down for over five days.

It wasn't until Dick got into his 50's that we began to have trouble with him and medical emergencies and I would tell him that I couldn't wait for him to grow out of the terrible 50's! Dick was taken to the hospital for a broken thumb after flying a neighbor, who had a broken shoulder, out to the highway so he could be transported to town. I drove the injured man's snow machine to the highway along with his wife on her machine. When we were loading the snow machines on their trailer the hand winch broke suddenly leaving the handle spinning very fast. Dick reached for the handle without thinking and it smacked his gloved hand blowing his thumb apart. Thankfully he had a good glove on that held onto the thumb so it could be put back together again at the hospital. This was one of those emergencies where Dick went to the hospital along with the original injured man. Dick had a steel pin put in his thumb and his hand was in a cast for many weeks.

The next year we were out cutting firewood in the middle of winter and after Dick started his chain saw the cutting chain was frozen. Instead of hitting the chain on a log to loosen it up and run correctly Dick reached out with a gloved hand to flick the chain which took off immediately cutting a large gash vertically down his wrist. He stopped his saw and walked over to me saying, "Medic I need help". Oh how I hated to hear him say medic as that always meant real trouble. We went into our cabin where we took off his outer snow gear and I proceeded to use Q-tips and peroxide to clean wood chips, chain oil and other debris from the jagged cut. I could see all his ligaments to the fingers and everything still worked and no major artery was hit but the cut was far beyond my repairing ability. So we bandaged his arm as best as possible and headed for town on a snow machine. Since it was Dick's throttle hand he could not drive but we took his larger wide track machine and I drove with him sitting behind me. We had several feet of snow that year and the trail was hard packed but very narrow. With two people on the machine it was more difficult to steer and I did not get far from home before I was off the trail with the machine on its side and stuck. Now Dick could not help me so I proceeded to dig out the front end tub from snow, pack the snow in front of the skis a bit and then stand on the up hill side of the machines running board to yank the machine into an upright position. This worked out quite easy really. We were on our way again in only minutes. I managed to get stuck another time but was getting faster at the recovery. When we had driven about a third of the way to the highway we came across another couple, who were neighbors but quite a bit older, and they were off the trail stuck very badly. We just couldn't leave them stranded and getting more exhausted by the hour so we stopped to get them back onto the trail and running again. Alice noticed that Dick was holding his arm up in the air and asked him why and when he explained that was to slow the bleeding down because he cut his wrist with a chain saw and we were on our way to the hospital for repairs, poor Alice almost fainted. I then noticed that blood had seeped completely out of the huge mitt we had on Dick's arm so we added more bandages from sterile sanitary pads that Alice had with her emergency kit and used an ace bandage to hold them in place which worked just great. Remember that one if you ever have an emergency with a lot of blood loss.

The worst shocker was June 2002 when Dick quit working in the middle of the day and told me we were going to town immediately. When I asked him why he answered, "Well don't be alarmed but I think I am having a heart attack." That got my attention right away and we proceeded to close up our cabin quite fast. Dick was so stubborn that he would not let me drive the boat to the highway and I was scared to death of him passing out on the way down river. He did quite well on the journey to the doctor's office where he was examined and put in the hospital immediately. The next morning his was medi-vaced down to the city of Anchorage where he had a stint put in. I drove in record time to Anchorage, a 6-7 hour drive, where I found Dick already out of the surgery and into a room looking great. He managed to follow doctor's orders to remain idle for a week and then Dick resumed his normal wood cutting and construction projects. You just can't keep a good man down!

We had so many times that we used our airplane, or double wide snow machine or our boat to haul different people down to the highway for transportation to the hospital. We were just glad to have the right equipment to make the transports more easily for everyone. The worst one was hauling a man out that broke his back after falling from a loft in a cabin and striking the edge of the kitchen counter with the middle of his back. That was a boat trip where we called ahead and had an ambulance waiting at the highway to pick up the injured man. The ambulance was backed down to the waters edge where we pulled in close and made a transfer from our boat directly into the back of the ambulance. This worked perfect for everyone with the least amount of movement to the injured.

So far everyone injured that we have helped managed to get repaired and went on to enjoy a fun outdoor lifestyle again. We have had a few that have died on this river but we were only a part of one of these incidents and he was already dead when Dick arrived. Dick and another neighbor sat out with his body for many hours through the night as they waited for a coroner to arrive. This was to keep any wild animals from the body before an investigation was done by the authorities.

Dick and I have both had advanced medical training for first aid over the years due to being in the Volunteer Fire Department years ago and because we chose to live far away from medical help. We have even taken suturing classes at our local hospital in Fairbanks but thankfully have never used that knowledge on anyone. It sure helps to be a little trained in first aid when you have a family that depends on you mostly.

We have been firm believers in the statement "live where you most want to live and take care of yourself and everything else that is important in life will happen along the way." Even as we grow older we do not want to base our life on being close to a hospital or existing in a nursing home facility. Thankfully we have both been able to maintain a fairly healthy life. That is not to say it has all been perfect as I have battled cancer, had knee and shoulder surgeries and Dick has had his share of heart problems twice in the past few years but we never give up or give into living in a city.

So far it has all worked out fine for us and we hope to have many more years enjoying the wild life. There is nothing like watching the many types of animals, depending on where you are located, as they are born, grow into maturity, forage for survival and play with one another in mock battles. We have had foxes like pets in our yard daily, squirrels that we feed by hand, birds of many types landing on our shoulders to eat which all entertain us in their own way. Moose wander through the yard year around. Watching the cows with their calves is so touching as the mothers guide the young ones in survival. We have had wolves circle our yard giving us the satisfaction of safely watching them. These things we have shared with our family over generations now. Who could ask for anything more peaceful and loving?

We wake up to the glorious sounds of birds, wind, rain and the river flowing only 125 feet from our doorway. When you view the beauty of nature at its best every single day and have the luxury of living among it all it becomes more than worth the bit of extra effort one puts out to live like this. Thankfully we have been able to do so for the better part of the past 50 years.

I only hope that we are able to share all of this for many more generations.